ALWAYS
TAKE
THE HIGH ROAD

IN YOUR PROFESSIONAL, PERSONAL, AND FINANCIAL LIFE

WRITTEN BY
JUDY BARKER AUSTIN

All rights reserved. No part of this book may be reproduced in any form or by any means, without permission of Judy Barker Austin

FIRST EDITION 2015

ISBN – 13:978-0692507858
(CUSTOM UNIVERSAL)
ISBN – 10:069250785X

BIASC: Self-Help/Motivational & Inspirational

JUDY BARKER AUSTIN
P. O. BOX 94
CENTERVILLE, IA 52544
judybarkeraustin.highroad@gmail.com

Also authored by Judy Barker Austin:

Available at

https://www.createspace.com/5682690

or amazon.com

Also authored by Judy Barker Austin:

Things My Mama Said

Available at:

https://www.createspace.com/6015715

Or at amazon.com

DISCLAIMERS

For as long as I can remember, I have written down inspirational and informative things I thought about on whatever I readily had available at the time whether it was in notebooks, on pieces of scrap paper, on the back of checkbooks, church programs, receipts, etc. Throughout my 30+ years of teaching and supervising educational, private business, governmental, and non-profit organizations, I have also collected and written down things I have experienced, read, or listened to. I then used and modified them in my professional and personal life. This book is very much a compilation of those thoughts and experiences. I made a decision in 2007 to share many of them with you. I do not remember from where much of my information originally came. Therefore, I am unable to document that information.

I realize some of you may not fully appreciate my spiritual references, but it would be impossible for me to write about my opinions and experiences on how to Take The High Road without including them. On the other hand, I know there will be some of you who believe I should have included even more spiritual examples than I have.

ACKNOWLEDGEMENT AND THANKS

This book is dedicated to all the people who have experienced workplace bullying and were able to Take The High Road to rise above their circumstances.

Thanks go to my children (Stephen, Jennifer, and Katie) for your research, writing, and proofing contributions and to my friends and family for all your encouragement.

I especially thank my parents, Tam and Buford Barker, who always believed in me, loved me, and made me feel I could accomplish all my dreams.

Every great dream begins with a dreamer. Always remember you have within you the strength, the patience, and the passion to reach for the stars to change the world.

~~~Harriet Tubman

PREFACE

I began to feel a "calling" in 2007 to write a book to put an end to workplace bullying after working in an environment where it was covert and obvious on a daily basis. As I researched and studied the topic, I found the material so depressing I knew I had to get the message out in a different manner.

One morning I was emotionally devastated after reading a news article about a hard-working and vibrant young worker who committed suicide because she was bullied. To take a break and compose myself, I went for a walk around a nearby park. As I strolled along, I glanced up to my right and noticed a higher road above me where cars traveled and other people walked. I snapped a mental photo of that vision and took it back with me where I later remembered how I had often advised others in My Professional and Personal Life to "Take The High Road." A light turned on liberating my mind and showing me how I should be positive and inspire others to Take The High Road, instead of demanding them to stop being a bully. After all, someone who travels on The High Road would not stoop so low as to become a workplace bully.

That afternoon when my daughter came home from school, I asked her, "What does Taking The High Road mean to you?" Without hesitation, she said, "When people do bad things to you, and you don't sink to their level--you rise to The High Road."

Later, I visited a state office I used to directly supervise and announced to the employees I was inspired to write about how to Take The High Road. When I asked their definition of the term High Road, Allison said, "the honest road–the safest one," while Mark intrigued me with his answer of, "no friction--harmony."

I used an online search engine and entered "high road" to discover the first edition of *Roget's New Millennium*™ *Thesaurus*, gave "ethical or easiest course" as the definition. I immediately thought *this can't be--it can't be the <u>easiest</u> course*. Taking The High Road is the harder road, not the easier one. This led to my revelation that "Taking The High Road" means different things to different people.

As I continued to contemplate the meanings and nuances of what "Taking The High Road" meant, I thought about how Taking The High Road to me had originally meant acting, looking, and thinking a little better than what you first want to do or what others expect you to do in a <u>certain situation</u>. It still seemed to fit, but I sensed it was much more. Instead of only Taking The High Road in isolated situations when stress or problems arose, I surmised whether or not it was possible to incorporate Taking The High Road in every aspect of life, all the time. I decided it could and should be attempted.

My "calling" then changed for me to write to inspire me, as well as others, to Always Take The High Road in all areas of Our Lives--Professional, Personal, and Financial.

Judy Barker Austin, 2015

Part One –
Introduction to
The High Road

<u>Chapter One</u> - When You Come to a Fork in the Road, Take The High Road, Page 11.

<u>Chapter Two</u> - A Road is Always Better Than a Path, Page 21.

<u>Chapter Three</u> - Listen to Elvis and Man of La Mancha (Follow Your Dreams), Page 29.

<u>Chapter Four</u> - Keep Your Motor Tuned and Tires Balanced (Have a Balanced Life Mentally, Emotionally, Physically, and Spiritually), Page 43.

<u>Chapter Five</u> - Beware of Pesky Potholes (Don't Get Discouraged), Page 63.

CHAPTER ONE - WHEN YOU COME TO A FORK IN THE ROAD, TAKE THE HIGH ROAD

Life is about decisions and choices. Shad Helmstetter wrote a book about choices and pointed out how when we live our lives by making our own choices, we have great freedom. I totally agree with Mr. Helmstetter's assessment.
You chose to open the pages of this book. You chose to start reading words from this book. Since you made those choices, you can use your great freedom to choose to make a lifelong commitment to "Always Take The High Road" in all areas of your life.

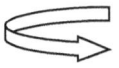 **HIGH ROAD HINT #1 – MAKE A COMMITMENT TO ALWAYS TAKE THE HIGH ROAD IN ALL AREAS OF YOUR LIFE.**

Can you have meaningful relationships without demeaning and mistreating family and friends? Is it possible to achieve Professional success and respect without bullying those around you? Can you flourish financially without lying and cheating? Can you find increased satisfaction in Your Spiritual Life? I passionately believe the answer to all the above questions is "yes."

You cannot be lost on a road that is straight.
~~~ A Proverb

I suggest you examine your everyday actions in a new way. As you read my examples of individuals who have Taken The High Road, I hope they inspire you to imitate their behavior in Your Professional, Personal, and Financial Life to help establish and maintain Mental, Emotional, Spiritual, and Physical balance.
I once worked as an area supervisor in a government agency where I was repeatedly asked for advice. Sometimes my answers centered on how to deal with co-workers, supervisors, and subordinates--and other times on how to deal with clients. After listening to a scenario, I often replied by saying, "Take the High Road." After a while those whom I had counseled more than once started saying, "I know. I know. Take the High Road." I expected when coming to a Fork in the Road, they would decide for themselves, given their unique situation, what was the most ethical thing to do, and then follow through with their decision. I expected their behavior to rise

above what I, or others, expected. Usually, I was pleased; sometimes I wasn't. Occasionally I was disappointed with the path they chose.

There are times when it's easy to Take The High Road and times when it's more complicated. You may even wonder what's in it for you if you try to take it, or if it's even worth the effort to try. The Low Road is often very inviting and enticing.

DONNY - Donny Deutsch, advertising executive and TV personality, believes we should Take The High Road because it's about a person's trust. I read once where he encouraged young people to be good. He even went on to say being good could turn into good money.

When we habitually Take The High Road, Our Professional and Personal Lives and relationships are nurtured. For me, Taking The High Road means you act in a way in every moment of your life higher than what *you* or *others around you at the time* expect.

If you don't want anyone to know, then don't do it.
~~~A Chinese Proverb

For example, when I was a teenager, my father was in law enforcement, and we lived in a small town in northwest Alabama located in a dry county. If a county is dry, it is illegal to sell or consume alcoholic beverages there. So as a teenager I had a triple whammy against me as far as drinking alcoholic beverages was concerned. I was under age, lived in a dry county, and my father was Buford Barker, the Chief of Police, who walked tall and carried a big stick. Therefore, I set very high standards for myself. (Even higher than what others expected of me.)

When I first attended college in Tuscaloosa, Alabama, I was 19, which at that time was the legal age to drink. Even though I was of age and now living in a wet county, I still felt I should be an example to those around me who knew me and knew my dad. So in college, I did not drink. I did this because I felt compelled to Take The High Road in everything I did and said; I wanted my dad to be proud and feel I represented my family name well.

WAYNE - I remember a scenario involving a boy named Wayne that occurred in my 8th-grade year. I was among a group of kids listening to a story he was telling about what some older kids had done definitely not connected to Taking The High Road. As an afterthought, Wayne turned to me, looked me in the eyes, and said, "But of course, Judy, you'd never be part of anything like that--you're Buford's daughter--you're a 'good' girl." I took this as a compliment, and it made me feel good. I saw admiration in the eyes of someone older and cooler. The remembrance of this scenario through the years proved to be a moral compass for me as I played it back time after time in my mind. I can picture his face and that moment to this day. I'm sure Wayne had no idea the impact his words had on me, and he probably doesn't even remember me.

Given the situation, sometimes your standards are higher, and sometimes the standards of others are higher. It changes. It vacillates. This means you should have a very clear vision and understanding of your personal standards, as well as an understanding of what others expect of you.

Taking The High Road when you're in a dilemma is a good thing, but could you take it a step further? Could you commit to **Always** Take The High Road when you come to a Fork in the Road? Not only when you encounter certain situations and not only in some areas of your life? What about in **every** aspect of Your Life--Professionally, Personally, and Financially?

NORMAN - Dr. Norman Vincent Peale, who wrote *The Power of Positive Thinking*, didn't say to think positive thoughts only in solitary circumstances or to get through one isolated situation and then never be positive again. He wanted it to be a permanent part of your life's journey.

I didn't write to help you to Take The High Road once or twice or even three times. My desire is for you to be in control and to direct your life, not allow it to direct or control you.

STAN AND TOOKIE - I do not believe you can ever be too bad to start on The High Road or it can ever be too late for you to start. If you beg to differ, read the following story about **Stan** and **Tookie** and then see if you feel the same. It's a story about choice, decisions, and Forks in the Road. Let's start with **Stan**.

Stan began his journey on The Low Road at a very early age. As a young boy in Shreveport, Louisiana, he believed if you wanted something, you had to take it and then fight to keep it. He stole food and toys, even though his mother and grandmother had taught him right from wrong. When little Stan was six, he boarded a bus with his mother, left his grandmother behind in Louisiana, and headed to California on what his mom thought was The High Road to prosperity.

Stan arrived in Los Angeles and continued to make inappropriate choices and avoid The High Road his mother so desperately wanted him to follow. He loved her, but he wouldn't listen to her and failed to show appreciation for her sacrifices. He was attracted to mischief in his elementary and middle school years which kept him on a Low Road filled with fighting and stealing.

When others offered to help him climb up to The High Road, Stan refused and chose to view himself as a "slave to self-hate." He was extremely intelligent but skipped school and made poor grades. His mother was kept busy finding a school that would accept him after he was kicked out of his former ones time and time again.

He had the abilities to sing and draw but did nothing worthwhile with the talents God gave him. He stayed on The Low Road and refused to take responsibility for his own actions. As a result, he never felt he experienced happiness as he grew up.

Seek and destroy became his motto, and at the youthful age of 17 Stan co-founded a violent gang in Los Angeles called the Crips, known for robberies and illegal drug sales. They attacked and killed anyone who got in the way of their criminal activities, even the innocent. Soon Crips were everywhere, day and night. Los Angeles radio stations took The Low Road and glorified the gang as they played a song about the Crips called *Crip Dog*. This gang and its fiendish activities spread throughout the United States and metastasized in South Africa. Over 30 years after Stan formed the gang, a district attorney in Los Angeles said, "This gang is responsible for the regular commission of crimes such as murder, rape, robbery, and drug sales."

You can't walk in the middle when you come to the Fork in the Road. Get ready to choose your side.
~~~Unknown Author

If Stan's mother had known how things would turn out for her son, she probably would have stayed in Shreveport and never boarded the bus to travel The Low Road to Los Angeles. Now let's talk a little about **Tookie**.

Tookie was a son who made his mother proud because he chose to travel The High Road and co-write a series of books called *Tookie Speaks Out Against Gang Violence*. This series included nine children's books promoting non-violent alternatives to gang violence. They have been used in classrooms all over the country. At one time, Tookie received 20-30 letters a day from supporters and children who had read his work. He wrote his autobiography, which was later used in Chicago's public school district's curriculum for at-risk students. Tookie donated money from his book sales to various charities such as Mothers Against Gang Wars. He continued to make good choices on The High Road as *Tookie's Corner,* an Internet education program founded by the Institute for the Prevention of Youth Violence, was developed.

Stan, on the other hand, encouraged more and more impressionable youths to follow him on his Low Road journey with the Crips. He was not moved to cry as boys in his gang were murdered. Instead, he was desensitized by all the ruthlessness he had experienced. He lashed out at the world and felt no empathy or remorse for them or their families. When he stared at their corpses, they were merely flashes of his future he couldn't face or feel. One of his homeboys was murdered because of his resemblance to Stan, and Stan lacked the humanity to even mourn the boy's death.

The Low Road got lower and lower until Stan was arrested at age 25 for murdering four innocent people in two separate robberies allegedly netted him less than $300. Two years later the guilty verdicts were read; Stan called the jurists "sons of bitches" and declared he would get even with them. When asked to cooperate with officials to bring other gang members to justice and stop gang violence, he refused to cooperate. He believed doing so was a violation of prison code. He felt the end result would be more violence for him and other inmates. While in prison on death row, he continued to associate with fellow Crips members and was part of the Blue Note Crips.

Tookie continued his journey on The High Road by helping mediate a peace agreement between two gangs involved in one of the deadliest gang wars in the history of the United States. The two gangs were called the Bloods and the Crips. His *Internet Project for Street Peace* linked high-risk youth in other countries to their counterparts in the United States in a peer-mentoring program. He wrote a *Local Street Peace Protocol*, which could be downloaded from *Tookie.com* to provide guidance on how to initiate a gang truce.

Stan was asked why he killed Albert Owens, a veteran, and father of two young girls. According to court records, Stan told friends he "didn't want to leave any witnesses." A fellow gang member of the Crips testified Stan told him he killed Owens "because he was white, and he was killing all white people." Stan was said to have made fun of Owens' death by laughing about the sounds he made when dying. The district attorney in rebuttal during the trial asked the question, "What man later laughs when he tells his friends how the victim gurgled as he lay dying?"

The answer to the district attorney's question seems fairly simple. The man who would do that has made corrupt choices and is on the lowest of Low Roads. It was also reported Stan called his other three victims *Buddha Heads* because of their Asian ancestry.

Tookie was on the highest of High Roads when he received the *Call to Service Award* and was commended for his social activism by President George W. Bush.

Stan continued on The Low Road as he was involved in a violent fight with another inmate after only two months in prison. He continued to assault fellow inmates as well as threaten guards. Because of this violent behavior, Stan spent six and one-half years in solitary confinement. At no time on death row did Stan ever admit to officials he killed the four people he was convicted of murdering.

Tookie was nominated for the Nobel Peace Prize five times and the Nobel Prize in Literature four times. He was nominated by many individuals who included college professors and a Swiss lawmaker. He also wrote a book about his life and was honored with a movie about him starring Jamie Foxx.

Stan was executed by lethal injection in California on December 13, 2005, and so was **Tookie** . . .

Stanley "Tookie" Williams was the second inmate executed in 2005, as he was denied clemency. In an interview with Tavis Smiley three weeks before his death, Williams said he was sorry for the losses of the Owens and Yang families, but he was innocent of their murders. He believed God had punished him for other things he'd done in his life. He also shared with Smiley how prison had allowed him to "read, learn, and grow." He had changed from a man "filled with rage" to a man whose life "revealed redemption."

During his time in solitary confinement, **Stanley "Tookie" Williams** got on The High Road and for the last 12 years of his life was able to influence the world for good.

Let's examine 10 important points inspired by the life of Stanley "Tookie" Williams.

1. WHEN YOU'RE ON THE LOW ROAD, IT AFFECTS YOU AND OTHERS IN NEGATIVE WAYS.

By following The Low Road, **Stanley "Tookie" Williams** spent 24 years on death row and was executed by lethal injection. On The Low Road, Stan Williams influenced young men to join gangs, deal drugs, rob, and murder. His actions cost Albert Owens, Yen-I Yang, Tsai-Shai Yang, and Yee-Chen Lin their lives, even though he may not have been the actual person to have murdered them. Albert Owens' two young daughters lost their dad. Robert Yang lost his father, mother, and sister. What has being on The Low Road cost you and those you influence?

2. YOU CAN GET ON THE HIGH ROAD NO MATTER HOW LOW YOU ARE ON THE LOW ROAD.

Stanley "Tookie" Williams co-founded a gang that ended up in almost all of the U. S. states and across the ocean in South Africa. He was executed for the murders of four people. He plotted to kill others while in prison. Can you plunge much lower than this?

 **HIGH ROAD HINT #2 - YOU ARE NEVER TOO LOW TO GET ON THE HIGH ROAD.**

At one point in his life, Stan decided to seek redemption and get on The High Road. He had spent six and one-half years in solitary confinement to come out a changed man and denounce his affiliation with the Crips. He could never take back or make better all the malevolence he'd committed but was determined to show some benevolence and accomplish something positive. He believed he had experienced what he called a "redemptive transition."

He felt he had earned the right to "both live redemption and to speak on it--even at the risk of being rejected and repudiated by the world." Do you believe you can get on The High Road no matter what you've done? Do you believe others can?

3. WHEN YOU GET ON THE HIGH ROAD, THE EXPERIENCE WILL AFFECT YOU AND OTHERS IN A POSITIVE WAY.

WILLIAM - William Glasser, known for his Reality Theory, believes there are two main things people search for in life.

One is the need to be loved unconditionally while being able to love in return.

The second is to believe you've done something worthwhile with your life and have the assurance others believe so, too. This concept can also be seen in the book, *The Cider House Rules*, where there are many discussions about "being of use."

ELEANOR - Eleanor Roosevelt's mother referred to Eleanor as "granny." Young Eleanor never felt she was attractive or loved. One day she decided to stop trying to become something she wasn't. She decided she would become "of use." As a result, she did much to help her future husband, Franklin Delano Roosevelt, and people throughout the world. She chose a Fork in the Road that did not include wasting her time complaining about what she didn't have or would never have. What about you? Have you chosen a Fork in the Road allowing you to live a life where you are "of use?"

At the end of his life, Tookie received unconditional love and respect from children and former gang members all over the world who were inspired by his books promoting alternatives to gang violence. He felt he was "being of use" as numerous young men turned their lives around because of his courage. He felt a calling to help children avoid a life filled with death and prison.

As **Stanley "Tookie" Williams** traveled through his life, he encountered many Forks in the Road. For many years, he took the wrong Forks. Finally, he came to a Fork in the Road and decided to Take The High Road.

HORACE - Horace Mann, who has often been called the Father of American Education, once said, "Be ashamed to die until you have won some victory for humanity." At the end of his life, Tookie was able to feel he had accomplished something worthwhile and was not ashamed to die because he had won many victories for humanity.

What can you do to make your life more worthwhile when you see your Forks in the Road? Have you won "some victory for humanity?" Are you "being of use?"

4. FOLLOW THE GOLDEN RULE.

Treat others like you want to be treated. Show respect to everyone. Stan had very little compassion for others until he spent his time in solitary confinement. There he thought about how he had treated others and decided to follow the golden rule. We don't have to go through what he went through before we decide to respect those we come into contact with each day.

5. KNOW THE RULES, AND FOLLOW THEM.

No matter how important you think you are, or what situation you're in, there are always rules, laws, norms, etc. to follow. There are rules you need to follow where you work and where you live. There are rules to follow when dealing with your finances. Know them, and follow them. Not once or twice, but all the time.

Stan thought he was invincible and rules didn't apply to him. He soon found out even when he didn't pay the price for breaking rules at the time he broke them, they would eventually catch up with him.

6. LOOK FOR AND IMITATE OTHERS ON THE HIGH ROAD.

Learn from example. Even though I shared the example of what happened to Stan because he didn't Take The High Road, I have provided the good he also did. I will also share other positive examples in this book. Those positive examples include a variety of individuals Taking The High Road from various ethnic, social, and economic backgrounds. Imitate and learn from them, but don't ignore them.

Stan had positive role models around him but chose to ignore them. When we open our eyes to make the decision to want to learn from positive role models, it will amaze us how many there are around us each day.

7. LEARN FROM YOUR MISTAKES AND DON'T MAKE THE SAME MISTAKES AGAIN.

When you make a mistake, even a BIG one, shake it off. Then learn from it, and do not make the same mistake again. The true test of being on The High Road is not to be completely perfect and never make a mistake; it is to try to never make the same mistake again.

Once **Stanley "Tookie" Williams** made the decision to turn his life around, he never reverted back to his bad behavior to make the same mistakes he had already made. He shook it off as best he could and put all his energy into doing something positive. He learned from his mistakes and helped others to avoid similar ones.

8. DO AN HONEST DAY'S WORK FOR AN HONEST DAY'S PAY.

Look for extra things to do on your job when you have completed your work for the day. This will serve you much better in the long run than to seek negative things to think about or say about others.

Tookie looked for something honest to do by writing children's books to help others to not get into gangs. He realized when he put immorality, dishonesty, and negativity into his life, he ultimately got repaid with what he created for himself. So instead put goodness, honesty, and positivity into your life; it will be given back to you. It creates a cycle.

9. GET TO KNOW AND UNDERSTAND THE BODY LANGUAGE OF OTHERS.

A main goal of reading body language is to figure out if someone is in an uncomfortable or comfortable situation. If you're not able to read body language correctly, you could ignore signs you have offended or hurt someone. Sometimes we need to stop thinking about our own needs and be in tune with what is going on around us. Stan was more caught up in his own agenda to notice what was going on around him much less care about if someone was uncomfortable.

When you are able to accurately read what is going on around you, you are then able to act accordingly. This can potentially help you see problems before they become problems which can lead you to U-turn from an uncomfortable or bad situation to find yourself on a High Road detour.

10. LEARN TO GET ALONG WITH AND ACCEPT THOSE WHO ARE DIFFERENT.

There will always be someone around you who is older, younger, darker, lighter, bigger, smaller, richer, poorer, taller, shorter, smarter, or less smart. Learn to deal with it without feeling inferior or superior.

Do not hate blindly as Stan did. The gangs he was affiliated with divided races, social classes, and taught hate for those who were different. See everyone as they are and accept them.

If an understanding of all people is achieved, then we can all learn to get along. Once that happens, you can learn new things from the differences that once divided you. Good luck, and remember when you come to Your Fork in the Road, Always Take The High Road.

> May the road rise to meet you
> May the wind always be at your back
> May the sunshine warm upon your face
> May the rains fall soft upon your fields
> And until we meet again
> May the Lord hold you
> In the palm of His hand
> ~ ~ ~ *Irish Blessing*

* * *

COMMENTS AND NOTES ON HOW TO TAKE THE HIGH ROAD WHEN APPROACHING A FORK IN THE ROAD.

_____

_____

_____

CHAPTER TWO - A ROAD IS ALWAYS BETTER THAN A PATH

When we were kids, my oldest brother (Ronald) and I explored woods bordering the back and one side of our house. We were often gone for hours on our adventures. As we ambled through the brush and trees, we looked for paths to make our journey easier. Sometimes we found a path; sometimes we didn't. If we didn't find a path within a few minutes, we turned around, backtracked, and headed for home. If we found a good path, we trudged along to look for things we had never seen and hoped to end up in places we had never been.

We found unusual plant and animal life. On one escapade, we examined several different types and colors of moss growing on live tree trunks as well as dead ones scattered on the forest's floor. One Saturday we spent all afternoon mesmerized as we caught tadpoles to let them go, only to re-catch over and over again.

On some days, we were explorers like Lewis and Clark as we found and forged through small streams of water to encounter undiscovered land. Other days we were amateur anthropologists as we contemplated the former use of old, unearthed bottles, rusty eating utensils, and a slew of discarded odds and ends from the past. There was even the day we pretended to be federal agents after we found remnants of a moonshine still.

During one of our Lewis and Clark journeys, our path got narrower and narrower and then abruptly stopped. We were confident we would find it again, so we pushed our way through bushes, briars, and trees to rediscover this elusive path. After several attempts and many cuts and scratches, we realized we were lost and none of the original path was in sight. It seemed the more we looked for the path, the more lost we became. As the sun made its descent and it started getting dark, we began to panic. We wondered if we would ever find the path or get out of the woods. We imagined killer bobcats, ravenous bears, and giant rattlesnakes would follow us ready to pounce as soon as the last stream of light filtered through the trees. As our panic peaked, we pushed our way into a clearing where straight ahead and across a field was a road. Not only a road, but a paved road, and one we recognized. If we walked down this road, it soon connected to another road that connected to another road that would lead us home. We were elated and pleased to find a road. I realized then paths were nice, but roads are better, especially paved ones.

There are many Paths in Our Professional, Personal, and Financial Lives we can travel on, but The High Road is better. There are three paths I believe are the ones most frequently trodden.

As I show in my **FIGURE 1 - THE AUSTIN HIGH ROAD MODEL FOR PROFESSIONAL, PERSONAL, AND FINANCIAL LIFE,** they are the Political/Financial, Legal, and Ethical. They may occasionally get us close to The High Road, but they are only what they are--Paths. They are not a road, and they are not The High Road.

POLITICAL/FINANCIAL PATH

This is the easiest path to get on as it is the largest, more frequently traveled, and easiest to find. On this path, you will see more people and have more company than any other path.

Travelers who ride or walk along this path base their decisions and choices on whether or not it will make them money or allow them to acquire or keep a job or political office. They don't worry too much if they break a law or hurt someone. They even try to rationalize those indiscretions away by contemplating the monetary gain they will accumulate and how they could assist others with ill-gained money, job, or political office. Their actions represent a Path and not The High Road.

WINSTON - Sir Winston Churchill once declared some men change their political party because of their principles, while others changed their principles because of their party. This doesn't mean it's wrong or unhealthy to have money or to get elected to a public office. It means if you want to Take The High Road, it's better not to base Your Professional or Personal Life exclusively on the success of Political or Financial Paths. There are a lot of successful, ethical rich people. The difference is they base their passions on a more noble foundation than to acquire wealth or political power.

OPRAH - I believe Oprah Winfrey is an excellent example of someone who has achieved financial independence while traveling The High Road instead of merely walking a Financial/Political Path. In a speech to the American Women's Economic Development Corporation, she discussed her personal ten commandments. Number Eight on that list was, "If money is your motivation--forget it." In her speech, she continued to stress how the reason for her success was based on the desire to do good work; the pursuit of money was never her objective. I'm sure she has turned down propositions that would make her money because they were either illegal or unethical as she once said, "It took a lot of courage to take The High Road, but I would rather be significant with six million people watching a show with meaning, than everyone watching a show with no meaning."

**FIGURE 1
AUSTIN HIGH ROAD MODEL
FOR PROFESSIONAL,
PERSONAL, AND
FINANCIAL LIFE**

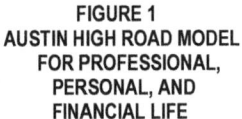

LEGAL PATH

The next Path is the Legal Path. Not as many follow this path as the Political/Financial Path. People traveling on this path, if faced with something that would promote them financially or politically, will at least ask the question, *"Is it legal?"* If it's illegal, they won't do it.

It's important to realize even though being legal and being ethical are often linked together, they are not the same. A Legal Path is closer to The High Road than the Political/Financial Path, but the Ethical Path is even closer. There are many things that are legal but may not be ethical. Abortion is legal, but many would not consider it an ethical choice. Not hiring someone because they are gay may not be illegal, but may be considered unethical.

TIM - You do not go to prison for ethical violations. If you don't believe it, ask Tim Montgomery. He'll tell you it's all about breaking the law. Tim Montgomery may have thought it was no big deal to help launder dirty money when he deposited bogus checks and received $20,000 for his assistance. He went to prison for his efforts. He discovered selling heroin and taking performance-enhancing drugs weren't good ideas either. It didn't matter he had two Olympic medals. It didn't matter he once had everything he had ever wanted in life and after setting a world record for running the 100 meters felt he had "stood at the top of the mountain."

He spent four and one-half years in prison, was released to a halfway house, and then sent home to confinement with an ankle brace and four years of probation. He worked to rebuild his life in Gainesville, Florida, coaching athletes of all ages through his company called NUMA Speed. In his first year, he built his client base up to 80. Hopefully, he's learned a lesson from his journey on The Low Road and will continue to head toward The High Road.

ETHICAL PATH

As previously stated, some things that are legal may not be ethical. If you're in business and you buy something from a supplier with terms of 2/10, n/30, you can get a 2% discount on your bill if you pay the balance within 10 days. If not, you have to pay the entire balance in 30 days.

If you instruct your office manager to wait and pay all bills on the 30th day, it is not illegal. Some may even look at that decision as a financially sound one. Yet some may see this as unethical as they believe you should pay the bill as soon as possible so as not to cause hardship on the company who allowed you some extra time to make payment.

Let me give you a personal example of something that happened to me that was not illegal but I considered to be unethical. I leased a house from a chiropractor in Florida who owned rental property. He allowed a representative (his girlfriend) to help manage his properties. Because of workplace bullying, I was forced to resign from my job and was looking for another job shortly after signing a one-year lease. For eleven months I was without a full-time job, but I faithfully made my payments without being late a single time.

When the lease expired, we had not negotiated a new lease because I had a possible job offer in Iowa. I sent in an extra one-month payment, and the representative said to let her know as soon as possible if I got the job. If I got the job, she agreed to refund the portion of the rent not used. I did get the job and immediately notified her.

A few days later she assured me she and the landlord would meet me to inspect the house and return my deposit and one-half unused portion of the rent. I waited for two and one-half hours on them as I called and left unanswered and unreturned voice mail and texts until I had my next door neighbor call from her phone. Once that happened, the representative answered her cell phone and agreed to immediately come to the house. When she arrived, she was alone and announced the landlord wasn't even in the state, and he would not return my half month's rent nor the deposit. She said, "Legally he doesn't have to give you the deposit until 30 days after he inspects the property, and I don't know when he's even going to be back in town."

What makes this an ethical issue is she knew the financial difficulties I was going through, being a single mom and not having a full-time job for 11 months. She also knew I had been bullied. There was nothing in the contract stating anything about me not getting my deposit back for 30 days.

The times we were in contact with each other after I let her know I would not be negotiating a new lease, she never mentioned there would be a delay in getting my deposit. If she had, I would have had time to make different arrangements concerning my move to allow for not getting my deposit back until 30 days later. This landlord's representative allowed me to wait on her and the landlord for two and one-half hours at the house. This was after I had already gotten everything out and cleaned it up, to then tell me she was not going to give me my deposit. She also had told me the landlord would be there to inspect the house when he wasn't even in town. She was not doing anything illegal, but she was not taking the ethical path. Someone who was on an ethical path would have made sure I got my deposit back to help me make a smooth transition in my move to another state. Not having my deposit to pay for a new place put me in a financial dilemma.

You might possibly assume I never got my deposit back, and you are right in your assumption. I never got my refund in rent or deposit back. I could have pressed charges against her and my former landlord because it was illegal for him to keep my deposit without a valid reason. It's my opinion they wanted to keep the money and believed since I was over a thousand miles away, I probably wouldn't press charges. The making me wait for two and one-half hours was an ethical issue. Not returning my deposit/refund morphed into a legal one.

Some things now illegal at one time were legal such as slavery, allowing children to work in horrible conditions in factories at times they should have been in school, and not allowing women to vote.

MARY KAY AND OPRAH - When slavery was legal, some people didn't own slaves because to them it was unethical. Also, many businessmen and women refused to hire school-age children during school hours--even though at the time there were no laws against the practice. Mary Kay Ash, the originator of Mary Kay Cosmetics, believed honesty was the cornerstone to all success; Oprah Winfrey considers real integrity to be doing the right thing when nobody even knows you did it.

MARK - Being on the ethical path as an employee often means going the extra mile to take care of your company's assets. You may not have to, but you do your part to make sure those entrusted assets are not broken, lost, or stolen. When I was looking at the human resources section of a website called ***about.com***, I found an interesting article by Mark S. Putnam entitled, *The Stuff of Work: Ethics and Assets*. In this article, he wrote about the importance of understanding who owns what and how to follow boundaries. You may want to read this article if it's still available online.

THE HIGH ROAD

The High Road is better than any of the three paths I mentioned. Even though my brother and I enjoyed discovering and traveling on paths, a road was superior.

To follow The High Road in Your Professional, Personal, and Financial Life will also prove superior to your journeys on Political/Financial, Legal, or Ethical Paths. Travelers on Paths are reactive; those on The High Road are proactive. Proactive means you look for ways to help others without seeking anything in return. The landlord's representative could have proactively not only given me my deposit and refund but brought me some Kentucky Fried Chicken to feed me and my daughter, as we had worked so hard to clean the house to get it ready for inspection we hadn't had a chance to get anything to eat. That would have been something proactive which would have been unexpected and highly appreciated.

PAULA AND JIM - Two examples of individuals who proactively Took The High Road transpired a few days after I arrived in Iowa. One individual had only met me a couple of hours before she found out I needed $100 to pay movers, who demanded cash, which I did not have, to move my furniture out of the rented moving van. She arrived without notice with the needed $100 and did not expect anything in return (except a repayment later) from her act of kindness. She even left her cell phone number and said if I needed more, for me to call her and she would drive to the closest ATM.

The next day a neighbor allowed me to borrow his cell phone for me and my daughter to use until we were able to change our cell phone coverage to a company able to provide proper service, as our current service was almost nonexistent.

The Iowan High Road kindness was refreshing after the Florida, *Illegal and Unethical*, Paths. I soon learned some people may be friendly, but there's a difference between being friendly and being a friend.

HIGH ROAD HINT #3 - THERE'S A DIFFERENCE BETWEEN BEING FRIENDLY AND BEING A FRIEND.

I am pleased to inform you those two High Road examples are Paula Mitchell and James D. Seddon, and they soon became close friends of mine.

Jim has since passed away, but his spirit is still with me as he encouraged my passion to help others Take The High Road. He shared what he had gone through to get his book written and published. *Morning Glories Among the Peas* is a memoir of his experiences in Vietnam, Cambodia, and Thailand, during the Vietnam War. I will always remember the day he dropped by my house with some homemade banana pudding (my favorite dessert) and an autographed copy of his book. Over a bowl of delicious banana pudding Jim said, "If I can write a book, so can you. Don't let anyone take away your dream."

Three things in human life are important: the first is to be kind; the second is to be kind; and the third is to be kind. ~~~Henry James

Thank you, Jim, for encouraging me to keep writing. Thank you, Paula, for letting me borrow $100, all you have continued to do for me, and for being one of my closest and dearest friends. Thank you both for being High Road examples of friendship.

(And I have to mention my other Iowa friends, **Lottie Wilson, Elaine Schweizer, Melissa Neher, Jan Swaby, Deb Becker, and Julie Mihalovich,** and all the others who later on helped me to fit into my work, community, and church environments.)

COMMENTS AND NOTES ON HOW TO FOLLOW THE HIGH ROAD INSTEAD OF A PATH.

_____

_____

_____

CHAPTER THREE - LISTEN TO ELVIS AND MAN OF LA MANCHA (FOLLOW YOUR DREAMS)

What do you listen to as you travel The High Road? Local and national news on the radio? Motivational messages or favorite songs on CDs or MP3 players? Do the things you listen to inspire you to be a better person and achieve your dreams? What are your dreams? Are they large enough for The High Road? How is your vision? Is it limited? A limited view can limit dreams.

A FROG - There was a frog at the bottom of a well. He looked up and thought the sky was only as big as the top of the well. The frog's dreams were small and he was unmotivated to do anything except to be unhappy and stay in the well because of his limited vision.

To dream, you must be motivated. I have taught motivation and motivation units in seminars as well as in an assortment of college-level Business and Psychology courses. I often introduce a unit or seminar with a story (probably not true) about a Texan with an unusual motivational strategy. The story goes something like this . . .

A TEXAN - A wealthy Texan held a private barbecue and invited 20 of the most eligible bachelors in the area. After a few hours of good food, drinks, and merriment, he gathered them around an Olympic-size swimming pool. "I guess you're wondering why I invited you to this barbecue," he announced. "As many of you know, I am a very rich man, and I have only one child, who is my lovely daughter, Clementine. Today is her 30th birthday, and I am seeking a suitable husband for her." All the bachelors glanced at Clementine and sighed, because she, at best, would be considered homely.

The Texan continued on to declare, "I have a task for you to measure your motivation. If you win and you're motivated by money, your prize is $1 million. If you're motivated by material possessions, your prize is 1,000 acres of my richest oil land, and if you are motivated by love, you win my stunning daughter's hand in marriage. Since she is my only heir, you will inherit approximately $3 billion." At this, the bachelors all looked at each other wondering what the task was, who would win, and what would be the winner's motivation. The Texan continued, "You see this swimming pool? It is filled with alligators, crocodiles, piranhas, leeches, and jellyfish. The first one to jump in and swim to the other side gets . . ."

Before the Texan could finish, a bachelor sprang into the pool and swam for his life with crocodiles, alligators, and piranhas in pursuit. The young man swam faster than Johnny Weissmuller, Mark Spitz, and Michael Phelps had ever swum--screaming and cursing as he flung off leeches and jellyfish attaching themselves to him.

When he reached the other side of the pool and pulled himself out, the other bachelors, the Texan, and Clementine ran to greet him. "I am so proud of you," said the Texan. "I have never seen such motivation, young man. Are you motivated by the $1 million?" The young man was hunched over and breathing so hard he could hardly speak but managed to whisper, "No sir."

The Texan then said, "Are you motivated by the 1,000 acres of prime oil land?" Again the young bachelor whispered, "No sir."

The Texan smiled and said, "If you're not motivated by money or material possessions, you must have swum so hard and so fast under such overwhelming obstacles because you were motivated by love. Do you want to marry my daughter?" The bachelor declared, "No sir. Right now I'm not motivated by money, material possessions, or love. What motivates me is to find out the name of the sorry rascal who pushed me in the pool."

I use this story to encourage a discussion about how each individual's motivation is different. What motivates you may be entirely different than what motivates your neighbor, your friend, or your family member. You may think you know a person's motivation--but you never really do.

Dreams are wishes your heart makes.
~~~An American Proverb

What motivates you? What inspires you? What is your passion? I'm a firm believer if you enjoy what you do and it's your passion, it's easier to get on The High Road and stay there. This involves selecting a job or career connecting you with something you really care about and can do well.

DAVID - Dr. David McClelland, former Professor and once Head of Harvard's Psychology and Social Relations Department, thought it was good to understand our motivation. If we didn't, he felt we would waste time chasing unnecessary rainbows to be unfocused. Dr. McClelland believed there were three main motivators and one is a more dominant motivator to every individual.

The three motivators are Achievement, Affiliation, and Power. In a graduate management course I took at the University of Alabama, my professor gave us a short version of the McClelland test used to determine dominant motivation. When I received my score, I found I was equally Achievement and Affiliation-oriented with no Power tendencies. Sometimes, I gave a similar test to my management students who found it interesting to know in which area they scored the highest.

ACHIEVEMENT-MOTIVATED

These individuals are the type who are successful when they go into business for themselves. They prefer working alone and are motivated to set up and accomplish risky, but obtainable goals.

AFFILIATION-MOTIVATED

If faced with competition, Affiliation-motivated individuals will favor collaboration. They are not mainly motivated by high risk or uncertainty. They are motivated by being liked and belonging to a cohesive group. If you're an Affiliation-motivated person, you work well in an environment filled with people who get along well with one another. You probably don't want to stand out or be in situations where you are required to order others around.

POWER-MOTIVATED

They enjoy being right and having an opportunity to control and influence others. They are motivated by competitions and the chance to win those competitions. They like to win arguments and bask in the rays of status and recognition. Most CEOs of large businesses or corporations are motivated by power and enjoy telling others what to do and then watching them do what they were told to do.

The measure of a man is what he does with power.
~~~Plato

I often assigned students in teams to accomplish tasks for learning activities. I walked around the classroom and listened in on each team's interactions and quickly discovered into which of the three categories of McClelland's theory that students should be placed.

Power-motivated students would tell other students what to do and then lean back satisfied with a smile on their faces as they watched their teammates, in fact, do what they had been told to do.

Affiliation-motivated students loved to be in a group. Often they paid no attention to the task at hand and were more motivated to talk to each other about what they had done the night before and what they planned to do after class. I heard them talk about the last party they had attended, who had been there, and how much fun they all had.

Achievement-motivated students were the most uncomfortable of the students in a group or team setting. They resented the Power-motivated students' attempts to try to tell them what to do and did not trust the Affiliation-motivated students to contribute anything worthwhile to the work needing to be accomplished. They wanted to, and often did, make a request to do all the work themselves. They didn't think anyone could do a job as well as they could.

I often saw evidence of these three motivations in my children. When my son was seven, I asked him to take some towels to the laundry room. Since he saved money to buy popular action figures, I agreed to deliver a nickel for his completed task. He soon called his four-year-old sister into the bathroom and offered her a dime if she would take those towels to the laundry room. She was glad to do so. Even though it took her several trips to complete her task, she proudly did so with a smile on her face. She fit the Achievement-motivated model because she enjoyed doing a job and doing it right. Her brother paid her the dime, and I paid him the nickel. Because he was Power-motivated, he was willing to pay twice as much as he had received to have the satisfaction of telling his little sister what to do and then watch her do it.

As I often told my students, I believe McClelland left out another type of motivation. At the time, I didn't know what to call it. I told them perhaps we could call it "Service" or "Do-Good" or "Being of Use" motivation. Now I know it should be called "High Road" motivation. It is where people are motivated to do something because they want to be of use or to help others.

TERESA - Why do you think Mother Teresa left the comfort of her home, and then her convent, to live among and become a servant to the poorest of the poor? It wasn't for Achievement, Power, or Affiliation. She didn't want her name to be recognized.

When she won the Nobel Peace Prize, she refused to attend the ceremonial banquet Laureates attended to be applauded for their accomplishments. She even asked for her $192,000 prize to be given to the poor people in India and declared earthly rewards were of use only if they could help the needy.

She had no motivation to tell others what to do, and most of the sick, poverty-stricken individuals she spent time with soon died before she was able to fully enjoy the time to be affiliated with them. Mother Teresa was motivated by Taking The High Road. Her motivation was fueled when she served others with respect, love, and dignity. She once said, "People who were forced to live like animals should die like angels--loved and wanted."

This concept motivates me to write. I do not want to tell people what to do. I am not concerned about seeing my name in print. I am not compelled to become an accomplished author so I can get together with acclaimed and talented authors to party and discuss our next endeavors like the Hemingways and Fitzgeralds of yesterday did.

I hope to motivate you and that frog (mentioned at the beginning of this chapter) to climb up the side of your well to see how large your world really is. That should have the end result of us working together to help the world be a better place in which to live.

WILL - Actor Will Smith, on the first episode of the Tonight Show with Jimmy Fallon, told Jimmy being an artist means you give to make the lives of others better and it should go outward and never be about you and your own needs. Maybe at this point in Will's life he has enough friends, money, and achievement and is looking for ways to help and inspire others through High Road motivation.

So--what motivates you? What is your dream?

I love to listen to Elvis Presley's passionate recording of the lyrics of *The Impossible Dream* composed and written for the 1965 musical, *Man of La Mancha*, by Mitch Leigh and Joe Darion. Even though reprised partially three times, the song is sung all the way through only once in the play. Don Quixote sings it as he stands vigil over his armor, in response to Aldonza's question about what he means by "following the quest." Elvis's rendition has always inspired me to never give up on my dreams, no matter how impossible they sometimes seem.

Do you love what you do? Is it your passion? Is it the type of work you always dreamed of doing? Do you participate in some way to do something good for others or make their lives better? If your answer is no, you may want to consider re-evaluating what you are doing or going to do to put and keep bread on your table.

Choose a job you love, and you will never have to work a day in your life. ~~~Confucius

LUCA - Luca Manfe won season four of the Master Chef competition. I can still visualize the excitement in his eyes when he won the $250,000 prize money as red and yellow confetti cascaded from the ceiling and Chef Gordon Ramsay sprayed Luca with champagne. Luca immigrated to America because to him it was the best place in the world to have dreams come true. He gave up a lot to come to follow the America Dream. Have you given up anything for your dream? Are you willing to give up anything for your dream?

SANDY, ART, AND BILL - Sandy Greenberg contracted glaucoma in college which left him legally blind. He probably would have dropped out of school if his roommate hadn't given up valuable study time of his own to read to him at night. Sandy finished his undergraduate studies and continued to graduate school. Even though he was poor and on financial aid, he had saved $500.

His roommate also continued to graduate school, but at another college. One day Sandy's former roommate called to share how unhappy he was and how he wished he could drop out of graduate school and do something else. When Sandy asked him what he wanted to do, the ex-roommate told him how he loved to sing and had a high school friend who played guitar. Their dream was to make a promo record. To do that, he needed $500. Without hesitation, Sandy gave his ex-roommate the needed $500.

This ex-roommate was Art Garfunkel, who took the $500, and teamed up with Paul Simon to cut a record which became *The Sounds of Silence.*

Art Garfunkel gave up a career he was not passionate about to pursue his dream. Because he Took The High Road and read to his roommate, his roommate in turn helped him reach his dream. I am so glad he did because Art Garfunkel and Paul Simon recorded *Bridge over Troubled Water,* which is one of my all-time favorite songs. This song soothed me and helped me through a lot of tough times during my high school years.

Sometimes you have to follow Art Garfunkel's example and give up something to follow your dream. What do you need to give up, or start to do, to pursue your dream?

When I taught college microeconomics and cost accounting classes, my students and I discussed how whatever is the best thing(s) we give up to get something else is called an opportunity cost.

Opportunity costs are not restricted to financial things. They can be anything that could give, or presently gives, us status or pleasure. Art's opportunity cost was a graduate degree (which he later obtained as well as a doctorate degree). Bill Gates gave up attaining a degree at Harvard to pursue his dream and later on started Microsoft. What opportunity costs will you incur to fulfill your dreams?

Not only do you need to give up something to accomplish your dreams, but you also need to do something. It could mean doing research on a career or a way to make money. You will definitely need to plan and set goals. Maybe you should take a personality or vocational test to see what line of work for which you're best suited. If it's worth dreaming, it's worth planning for. If it's worth planning for, it's worth writing down. The actual process of writing something down creates more oxygen flow to the area of your brain responsible for memories and even exercises that part of the brain. This is one of the reasons professors and counselors encourage us to keep a journal or blog.

This reminds me of a lady who asked her husband to go to the store to buy her some vanilla ice cream and wanted him to write it down so he wouldn't forget. "I can remember; I don't have to write it down," said her husband. As he walked out the door, she called out she wanted some chocolate syrup as well, but he needed to write it down. "I can remember vanilla ice cream and chocolate syrup without writing it down," he replied back. As he opened his car door, he heard her voice once again. "Honey," she said, "I have one more request. Could you please bring me some of those fancy, crushed nuts to sprinkle on top?" "I'd be glad to, my love," said her husband, patiently. As he drove off, she yelled out one last time, "Please write it down, darling." He didn't hear her, but in his mind all the way to the grocery store he was going over the list of what to buy his wife--vanilla ice cream, chocolate syrup, and fancy, crushed nuts to sprinkle on top--vanilla ice cream, chocolate syrup, and fancy, crushed nuts to sprinkle on top.

Guess what? You got it! When he walked into the grocery store, he forgot what he was supposed to purchase. Do you know what he did? He bought a dozen eggs because, after all, everyone always needs eggs. When he got home and gingerly handed his wife a bag with the dozen eggs, she looked in the bag and cried out, "You never listen to me. I told you to write it down. How do you expect me to make breakfast when you can't even remember to bring home the bacon?" Not only should he have written it down, but she should also have, too, for neither one remembered the original items.

The palest ink is better than the best memory.
~~~A Chinese Parable.

Write down your plan. Then realize if it's valuable enough to write down, it's valuable enough to put into action. What good is it to have a plan and write it down if you never do anything with it? Also, why spend time stressing out over something you're not doing, or going to do anything about?

HIGH ROAD HINT #4 – SPEND TIME IMPROVING YOUR SITUATION, INSTEAD OF STRESSING OUT OVER IT.

If you need help to write down your plan or put it into action, allow others to help you. Build up your support system of mentors, family, and friends. When you let someone else know about and help you with your plan, you become accountable and your chances for success increase.

To achieve your dreams, what do you think is the most important quality to have? You might think it should be high intelligence. If that's the case, why are so many highly intelligent individuals unable to reach their full potential or realize their dreams? Or why are there so many not-so-highly intelligent people successfully reaching their goals every day?

ANGELA AND MICHAEL - According to the March 1, 2014, issue of *Psychology Today*, University of Pennsylvania psychologist, Angela Duckworth, studied West Point cadets to discover the best predictor of success in completing Cadet Basic Training. She along with other psychologists discovered it was "grit" and not high intelligence. "Grit" represents an individual's capacity to successfully reach challenging, long-term goals. The cadets with a high grit score believed they could successfully complete training no matter how difficult it would be.

Dr. Duckworth also believed some of the grittiest people are community college students and how their grittiness ranks right up there with Olympic athletes and students obtaining advanced degrees. Since I have taught in a community college environment, I totally agree. Most students are focused on achieving their dreams to complete the necessary work to acquire their college degrees. Many work full time and are parents of small children. They incur multiple "opportunity costs" and decide they will acquire their degree no matter what they have to go through. They sacrifice and give up so much as they juggle commitments.

Michael D. Matthews, who wrote the *Psychology Today* article about Angela Duckworth's findings, was once a law enforcement officer. His combat shooting instructor had told him and other students if they died following a shootout, they should be found clutching a pistol with an empty magazine. This means you should give everything you have right up to the very end. Matthews was also quick to point out you must be realistic. (*So you might want to reconsider a dream to become a nuclear physicist if you hate math and make poor grades in it.*)

If you don't have a plan for yourself, you'll be a part of someone else's. ~~~An American Proverb

Set high goals, and be gritty. When you set a goal, you have a destination; you can detour right past The Low Road. As you set constructive and manageable goals, it becomes easier to stay on The High Road. Continually visualize your direction, because the follow through to reach a goal is not always black and white.

Here are 10 ways I believe can help you to stay on track to fulfilling a goal (not only setting a goal) in High Road terms.

1. KNOW YOUR DIRECTION, AND BE SPECIFIC ABOUT WHERE YOU WANT TO GO.

Where do you want to go? What do you want to accomplish? These questions must be answered to have a successful goal. Since you shouldn't start a trip before you consult a map or GPS, you shouldn't go through life unless you know which direction you want to take to achieve your goals. If you do not know where you want to go, you can put forth a lot of effort and get nowhere. When I teach seminars and classes about setting goals, I often use the following **SMART** acronym for guidance.

Specific - Sometimes to be specific enough, you may have to work on one major goal at a time. Your brain is like a bow and arrow constantly looking for a target. You work and feel better when you are fully engaged going after "clear" targets. If your target is vague or ambiguous, you become confused and either shut down or go after the wrong target.

Measured - What gets measured gets done. You can see your progress and if you are traveling in the right direction.

Attainable - To be attainable, your goals should be reasonable, achievable, and accomplishable. They should have an 80% or better chance of being attained, so don't make them TOO easy.

Relevant - Significant, realistic, and meaningful goals are goals that are relevant. Why set goals which if achieved aren't even significant or meaningful to you?

Trackable - Trackable goals have a natural ending as they are time-bound with clear deadlines. This, in turn, provides motivation and urgency.

2. TAKE ADVANTAGE OF OPPORTUNITIES AND SHORTCUTS.

A shortcut is not a short circuit. Sometimes an opportunity or shortcut will come your way which can save you a lot of time, effort, and money. Show courage, and take it.

3. KNOW YOUR ETA (ESTIMATED TIME OF ARRIVAL).

Have a set time to accomplish your goal. This will help keep your motivational level up.

4. MONITOR YOUR PROGRESS.

Keep up with how well you're doing in attaining your goal. Maintain a journal to document your progress as well as the obstacles you overcome.

5. HOPE FOR GOOD WEATHER, BUT PREPARE FOR BAD WEATHER.

Every trip on The High Road can have good and/or bad weather. Be aware you will encounter some rain or snow on the road as you accomplish goals. Have a plan for what to do when you encounter setbacks and appreciate and be thankful for the good weather.

6. PUT MORE IMPORTANCE ON YOUR GOALS AND LESS ON YOUR ACCOMPLISHMENT OF THE GOALS.

Remember why you set your goals in the first place. If you don't, you can get too wrapped up in the process and less in what the goals stand for.

7. BE GRITTY, AND KEEP ON TRUCKING.

THOMAS - Don't give up on your goals when the road gets a little bumpy. Thomas Edison once said, "I have not failed. I've just found 10,000 ways that won't work." Edison is a great example of a successful goal setter and completer. He was ridiculed and labeled unintelligent in school, but he stayed on The High Road and made dream after dream a reality.

HARLAND - Colonel Harland Sanders, the creator of the Kentucky Fried Chicken's famous chicken recipe, showed his grit when he finally reached his goal after being rejected over a thousand times. Now even some of the most rural cities have a KFC. He had a dream to "amount to something" and one day resolved to contribute however much time, effort, or money required to be sure he gave his best efforts to achieve that goal. He never gave up even though he tried a lot of things and failed at most of them. He even once had a job cleaning out ashtrays in trains in Jasper, Alabama. Because of his grit and determination he knew he was a winner.

8. DON'T SUCCUMB TO SELF-SABOTAGE.

When you set goals, you're on the right track. Always feel you are worth achieving whatever goal you set. Too many give up when their goal is within their reach and self-sabotage keeps them from taking that last step or finishing that last task. Minister and Motivator Joel Osteen speaks about this often when he shares that the closer we get to our goals, the harder the adversity is. So when things are really getting tough, it may only mean our goal is right around the corner.

Setting goals, while important, also has the ability to set you up to travel down wrong ways and dead ends. Self-sabotage is a misguided attempt at dealing with intense emotions. Self-sabotage is often referenced by the common saying, "You shot yourself in the foot." The idea of setting a goal too high may be seen as self-sabotage, but it usually is not the problem; so aim high! The problem is commonly the opposite--setting goals too low. This lack of self-worth is a type of self-sabotage in reaching goals, as well as procrastination and indulging in bad habits such as drinking, eating, smoking, and using other substances to excess. That is not the best way to ease negative emotions.

BRITNEY - An example of bad self-worth which led to self-sabotage can be found in pop star Britney Spears' life. She went from poor relationship choices to an extreme spiral when she shaved her head and showcased multiple public displays of poor judgment. Her low self-worth and sabotaging ways brought her down to The Low Road. Through setting appropriate goals and good family support, she was later able to get off Her Low Road and head toward a better road.

JAMES - Having appropriate goals and listening to advice from those who have been through bouts of self-sabotage can be helpful. I read in an in-flight airline magazine article singer/songwriter James Taylor has three points of advice,

(1) don't get into too much debt,
(2) don't be a slave to substance abuse, and
(3) don't start a family until you are ready to settle down.

These three areas can sabotage your life if not handled appropriately.

9. SEEK OUT INSPIRATIONAL ROLE MODELS.

Read, study, and apply the principles of individuals who inspire you. I recently took an online poll to find out what famous person most motivated me. I answered a series of questions about my likes and dislikes to find Walt Disney was my person of motivation. The survey revealed I viewed love and kids as being of high importance. It also said

I place great value on social things and have a lot of love to give. The quote given to inspire me was, "All our dreams can come true if we have the courage to pursue them."

CARL, HELEN, AND BEAR - Growing up in rural Alabama, I was inspired by fellow Alabamians, Helen Keller and Congressman Carl Elliott, as well as Paul "Bear" Bryant, football coach at The University of Alabama during my college years. Who inspires you? Why do they inspire you?

Congressman Carl Elliott is from my hometown of Vina, Alabama. He was the champion of poor, "gritty" people who dreamed of being a college graduate.

Helen Keller was born and raised in Tuscumbia, Alabama, approximately 40 miles from where I was born and raised. Even though struck blind, deaf, and mute around eighteen months old, she went on to graduate college (first deaf/blind person to do so) and travel to 35 countries on five continents speaking on behalf of the rights of women and people with disabilities.

Even at the age of 75, Helen was still going strong when she traveled over 40,000 miles during five months across Asia. She not only triumphed over her own adversities, but she also helped and inspired others. She died in her sleep a few weeks before her 88th birthday. I graduated from high school the year she was inducted into the Alabama Women's Hall of Fame, three years after her death. Her picture is on the Alabama quarter, and this quarter is the only one to have braille on it.

My favorite quote from Helen Keller is on my personal Facebook page which goes, "Keep your face to the sunshine, and you cannot see a shadow."

Paul "Bear" Bryant overcame poverty and adversity to win more college football games in the 1960s and 1970s than any other head coach. In over 38 years as head coach at The University of Maryland, The University of Kentucky, Texas A&M University, and The University of Alabama he had an overall record of 323-85-17.

Coach Bryant constantly told his players, coaches, fans, and media to never quit on a goal. He also stressed when we attain a goal, we should set another and start to work toward its attainment. He once said, "I don't want ordinary people. I want people who are willing to sacrifice and do without a lot of those things ordinary students get to do. That's what it takes to win." He was already 6' 1" and 180 pounds at 13 when a carnival barker propositioned him to fight a bear for $1 a minute. After fighting the bear who bit Bryant's ear, he never even received any money, but did acquire the nickname of "Bear."

After becoming a successful coach at The University of Alabama, Coach Bryant was often offered other opportunities like being an actor and the coach of the Miami Dolphins, both of which would have netted him a lot more money. He later said he was happy in Alabama and would never leave for financial reasons.

He died 28 days after coaching his last game. He was born on September 11, and in 2013 people celebrated what would have been his 100th birthday. As I watched an episode of *Law and Order*, I heard actor and former Tennessee Senator Fred Thompson (who was born in Sheffield, Alabama) say if it hadn't been for Osama bin Laden the date September 11 would only be known as Bear Bryant's birthday.

One out of every 12 Alabama citizens lined up and paid respect along the 55-mile route his body took traveling from his funeral service in Tuscaloosa, Alabama, to his burial spot in Birmingham's Elmwood Cemetery. John McKay, former USC head football coach, once remarked Coach Bryant wasn't only a coach but was *the* coach. Bear's mama always wanted him to be a preacher. He told her coaching and preaching were a lot alike.

10. CELEBRATE SERENDIPITY.

The definition of serendipity according to dictionary.com is "luck that takes the form of finding valuable or pleasant things that are not looked for." While it's a good idea to think about and read about people who inspire us, it's also a good idea to be aware of random, unexpected experiences that can give you *AHA* moments of inspiration.

I have two rings I often wear that boast inspirational inscriptions. One says, *be true to your dreams,* and the other one simply says, HOPE. When I bought these rings (on separate occasions, years apart) I was not specifically looking to be inspired. Yet because I am aware of and look for random, unexpected experiences to give me inspiration, I purchased the rings. When I wear these rings and look down at the words, I am inspired and motivated to continue to pursue my dream to motivate others to Take The High Road.

NOOR - I was home relaxing in front of my TV watching the 2012 Summer Olympics not expecting any inspiration when I saw Noor Hussain Al-Malki compete in track and field. The announcer reported she was Qatar's first female to compete in track and field in an Olympic game. She didn't win or even finish the race, as she was injured coming out of the blocks and taken off the track in a wheelchair. That's not what inspired and motivated me. What inspired me was learning the harassment and bullying she had endured before she got to the competition. In her country, a taxi driver told her to get out of the cab when he found out she was on her way to train for the London Olympics. She was constantly harassed during training, with men hurling insults at her telling her she couldn't win, how it wasn't her job, how it wasn't good for the men in her country for her to be seen there, and her place was to be behind her man. Through it all she did reach her dream to make it to the Olympics and inspire other women in her country to also compete.

Another random, unexpected moment inspiring me was when I took my teenage daughter to a Black Eyed Peas Concert in Des Moines, Iowa. The group consists of will.i.am, apl.de.ap, Taboo, and Fergie. will.i.am (William James Adams, Jr) closed out the concert by encouraging the audience to always follow our dreams, even when others make fun of our dreams and try to make us give them up. I was totally inspired by his sincerity and honest approach. It was a serendipitous moment for me and my daughter.

On Your High Road of Life, keep your radio tuned to Will.i.am, Elvis, and Man of La Mancha; NEVER, NEVER, NEVER give up on your dreams; and embrace serendipity.

* * *

COMMENTS AND NOTES ON
HOW TO LISTEN TO ELVIS AND MAN OF LA
MANCHA AND FOLLOW DREAMS.

_____

_____

_____

CHAPTER FOUR - KEEP YOUR MOTOR TUNED AND TIRES BALANCED (HAVE A BALANCED LIFE MENTALLY, EMOTIONALLY, PHYSICALLY, AND SPIRITUALLY)

It's usually easier to acknowledge someone else's problems than it is to acknowledge your own. If you need your motor tuned or tires balanced, will you admit it? Or do you continue driving until your motor catches on fire or your tires have a blowout? Blown-out tires and burned up motors not only ruin your trips in life--but also the trips of those around you.

People who are hurting, hurt people.
~~~Unknown Author

A man barged into a psychiatrist's office dressed like Napoleon Bonaparte, "Doctor, I need help right now," he yelled. "I believe you," answered the doctor. "Why don't you calm down, lie down on my couch, and tell me all your problems." "I don't have any problems, and I don't need to calm down," the man snapped. "I am Napoleon Bonaparte. I am the Emperor of France. I have everything I could possibly want--money, women, and power--everything! But I'm afraid my wife, Josephine, is in deep mental trouble." "All right," said the psychiatrist, humoring his distraught patient. "What seems to be HER main problem?" The unhappy man paused and then declared, "For some strange reason, she thinks her name is Mrs. Schwartz instead of Mrs. Bonaparte."

Maybe you've heard the expression, "You might be a redneck if-- and then you fill in the blanks with something like, "You might be a redneck if you mow your yard and find a car." Well, you might need a mental tune-up and your tires balanced if your name is Mr. Schwartz and you think you're Napoleon Bonaparte.

My youngest daughter's car once had a flat tire as she was driving home from work late at night. For her, it was a very scary thing to be all alone and unable to get where she needed to go. She had to get her tire changed. She didn't keep driving along pretending nothing was wrong. On The High Road of Life when we have a problem, we can't pretend it's not there. We have to take action. She called me, and I brought someone out to change her tire. (Notice I brought someone to change the tire. I didn't change it as I know my limitations.) As a traveler on The High Road of Life, it's so important to be proactive rather than reactive.

You don't want to be stranded on the side of the road because you didn't keep your vehicle serviced. You also don't want to be stranded on the side of the Road of Life because you didn't keep your body and mind serviced.

For your motor to be tuned and your tires balanced, you must pay attention to Your Mental, Emotional, Physical, and Spiritual Health.

MENTAL HEALTH

STEPHEN - Writer and lecturer Stephen Covey discussed in his book, *The Seven Habits of Highly Effective People*, the importance of having Mental Health in order is as important as learning to read. I believe here is where you ask the question, *Am I driving the car, or is the car driving me?*

 **HIGH ROAD HINT #5 – DRIVE THE CAR. DON'T LET THE CAR DRIVE YOU.**

Major and even minor Mental Health issues can drive us to abuse alcohol, cigarettes, and other drugs. I recently read on the Website for the National Alliance on Mental Illness (NAMI), 1 in 25 people in the United States experience severe mental illness each year. Of those, only 60% are being treated for their illness.

People with untreated mental illness visit a medical doctor twice as much as those who are treated. Not only will Your Personal Life benefit from good Mental Health, so will Your Professional Life. You will be a more productive worker with fewer accidents and fewer absences. When employers and business owners provide Mental Health coverage, they can increase workplace efficiency and productivity.

> **This life is crazy and I am sane;**
> **Amongst the living a world of pain.**
> **I find my toiling is done so in vain;**
> **When sanity dies, still the living remain.**
> **~~~Stone Ronson**

Many famous and successful individuals have received treatment and worked through such things as addictions, alcoholism, and drug abuse problems, as well as learned to control bipolar and schizophrenic conditions. At one time, they let issues drive them but reached a Fork in the Road where they chose to drive instead of having their cars drive them. A few examples are Oprah Winfrey, Britney Spears, Jennifer

Aniston, Demi Lovato, Chaka Khan, Drew Barrymore, Eric Clapton, Catherine Zeta-Jones, Jon Stewart, Matt Damon, Slash, Brian "Head" Welch, Carrie Fisher, Jean-Claude Van Damme, Linda Hamilton, Sinead O'Connor, Jane Pauley, and Mariette Hartley.

Unfortunately, there is a longer list of those who were not able to get in the driver's seat like writers Virginia Woolf, Edgar Allan Poe, Mark Twain, Jack Kerouac, F. Scott Fitzgerald, and Truman Capote; actors Vivien Leigh, River Phoenix, Philip Seymour Hoffman, Heath Ledger, Marilyn Monroe, and Cory Monteith; athletes Erica Blasberg, Michael Carl Baze, Derek Boogaard, Andy Irons, Edward Fatu "Umaga", Mickey Mantle, and Christopher Bowman; artist Vincent van Gogh; psychiatrist Sigmund Freud; business executives Brian Epstein and Howard Hughes; comedians Robin Williams, Lenny Bruce, Chris Farley, W. C. Fields, and John Belushi; President Franklin Pierce; singers Amy Winehouse, Michael Jackson, Elvis Presley, Chris Kelly, Jim Morrison, Billie Holiday, Hank Williams, Sr., and Whitney Houston.

The list goes on and on. Many of them committed suicide. Most of them died as a result of their illnesses; the others suffered professional alienation and personal tragedies throughout their lives because they were determined to and had learned to function in their dysfunction. Research them and read their sad, sad stories.

Then there's this couple . . .

They were the golden couple of their time. They were trendy, intelligent, charismatic, and attractive. They partied with famous people in New York, Paris, and Rome. The press loved them and followed them all around the world. The public also loved them and wanted to be them. Tennessee Williams wrote about their love for each other in his last play. But it's time to hear the rest of their story.

He saw his father go bankrupt and his family have to live on money from his mother's side of the family. She grew up privileged and spoiled.

He spent his entire adult life worried and depressed because he couldn't pay off his debts. She loved to party and always required the finest things of life.

He always considered himself nothing but a failure. She felt he held her back from the success she could have achieved by censoring her writing and not taking her painting and dancing abilities seriously.

Even though they lived all over the world in Switzerland, France, Italy, and six of the U.S. States, they never seemed to have a home. His best friend described their living conditions in Paris as "gloomy and airless, and nothing in it seemed to belong to them."

The golden boy was beaten by Italian police in Rome, involved in a drunken brawl and arrested several times in Paris, had numerous affairs in Switzerland, had an affair with a wealthy married guest from Texas while in North Carolina, had an affair with a 17-year-old child actress in California, made a scene at a famous producer's house in California which resulted in the loss of his job, and tried to stop a cockfight in Cuba which resulted in his getting beaten up by irate locals.

The golden girl refused to marry him until he reached a certain financial stability, burned her clothes in a bathtub of a prestigious Californian hotel, threw an expensive diamond and platinum watch out of a departing train, did cartwheels in a New York hotel lobby, danced on top of a kitchen table wearing a chef's hat in a restaurant, had an affair with a French pilot, flung herself down a flight of stairs because her golden husband showed too much attention to a famous dancer at a party, sprang out of her taxicab in Paris and ran through traffic in her ballet outfit, attempted suicide numerous times, and was admitted to mental hospitals in France, Switzerland, Maryland, and North Carolina.

They splashed their golden curls in the Plaza Hotel Fountain and rode on the roof of a taxicab down the streets of New York City. In Paris she announced over and over again she wanted a divorce, so he locked her out of the house until she no longer asked for one. She sabotaged his work, and he stole and censored hers. She hated his best friend and accused him and her husband of being lovers. This best friend hated her as well and called her vindictive, shallow, and crazy.

He tried to reinvent the one moderate success in his life but only got less and less successful as he sadly observed his famous friends get more and more successful. As a result, he spent most of his life in an alcoholic stupor. She was in and out of hospitals because of her mental illnesses for 18 years. They weren't capable enough to raise their only child and left that job to nannies, relatives, and institutions.

He died of a heart attack with his mistress as he ate a chocolate bar and listened to classical music. He hadn't seen his wife in one and one-half years. She died in a fire in a mental institution eight years later. They were both only in their forties at the time of their deaths.

He had to die so his life insurance policy could pay off their enormous debts. None of his works received anything more than modest commercial or critical success during his lifetime. Only after his death did he gain the reputation as one of the pre-eminent authors in the history of American literature. One of his novels went on to become required reading for virtually every American high school student for over 50 years.

She had to live her last years in a mental hospital to finally write and paint without being censored. Her novel sold less than a couple thousand copies in her lifetime (for which she earned less than $200), she never finished her second one, and her paintings were bizarre and anxiety provoking.

This golden couple never made it even close to The High Road because of his lifetime battle with alcoholism and her mental illnesses. They could not keep their engines tuned and their tires balanced.

He once wrote, "Here's to alcohol, the rose colored glasses of life." She once wrote, "It is the loose ends with which men hang themselves."

... He was F. Scott Fitzgerald, author of *The Great Gatsby*, and she was Zelda Sayre Fitzgerald, muse and love of his life.

The Betty Ford Center is founded on the belief alcoholism is highly treatable with great success, even though it is a mental illness. Information from their website warns of the complications of injuries and death if alcoholism is left untreated, or not treated properly.

F. Scott Fitzgerald never received any treatment for his alcoholism, nor did Zelda receive successful treatment for her mental conditions.

The magic and tragedy of their lives still speaks to us today through Fitzgerald's characters (many of whom were based on Zelda's struggles with mental illness) and the F. Scott and Zelda Fitzgerald Museum located in a house the golden couple once leased in a residential area on Felder Avenue in Montgomery, Alabama. It was in this house Zelda outlined her book, *Save Me the Waltz*, about a heroine named Alabama who is experiencing a breakdown in her marriage. F. Scott wrote his book, *Tender is the Night*, in that same house, which ironically is also about a bad marriage.

Below are some observations made and sent to me in an email from my daughter, Katie, after she visited the museum in Montgomery, Alabama.

"Zelda described Alabama's autumn in a letter to Scott, 'The weather here is a continual circus day--smoky with the sun like a red balloon and soft and romantic and sensual.'

With it being late August and fall closing in, I wondered if I was seeing the same sun she was as I followed the walkway that led to the front entrance of the F. Scott and Zelda Museum in Montgomery, Alabama. Before I reach the turn for the front door, I am stopped by a blooming magnolia tree that refused to go unnoticed. The tree's considerable size left me with no doubts if it wasn't maintained, it would surely take over the historic brick house. As I continue to gaze at the magnolia I see a thoughtfully placed bench at its trunk, and with that my mind traveled back to when F. Scott and Zelda could have been sitting there in the magnolia's shade. Possibly reading or writing together, having tea or coffee while talking about their day, deciding whether they'd go out to a party later, or arguing over some variety of marriage-like issues.

These thoughts ran through my mind as they do each time I go somewhere with such history. Once my curiosity of the magnolia waned, I started toward the stairs which brought me face-to-face with the front door of the Fitzgerald's Alabama home turned museum.

For a small donation the tour began. The tour guide led us into the lives of F. Scott and Zelda: the basics, the commonly unknown facts, and a look into deeper theories. The basics of their separate lives, marriage, writing, and family. Generally unknown facts of personal issues, mental health, and other art forms outside of writing were covered, too. Especially in regards to Zelda. Beneath her partying and superficial ways, she also had an artistic spirit. She enjoyed not only writing but painting, crafts, and fashion.

As I strolled through the museum, I saw spurts of her art in its various forms. There were whimsical, colorful paintings of flowers from her early work to more abstract paintings in her later work while she was living in a mental institution. Also, resting in a glass display case were small yet striking beaded purses she was known for spending her time making. Though F. Scott and Zelda had ups and downs in their relationship, highs and lows: it is rumored without this dynamic much of their work would never have taken form. They were each other's toxic muse."

At some point in time, we may eliminate the unfortunate stigma we have attached to mental illness. But until that happens, it's important to look to those who successfully manage their mental illnesses which include alcoholism and bipolar conditions. Bipolar disorder can be unnerving to friends, bosses, and family members who do not understand its dynamics. Sufferers seem normal until shifts in mood and energy take place. These shifts compromise the sufferer's ability to handle normal daily activities.

What should you do or what can you do to help someone with a mental illness like alcoholism, drug abuse, or bipolar disorder? I offer the following five suggestions.

1. **HELP THEM UNDERSTAND THEY MUST WANT TO BE HELPED.**

I believe the main reason people with mental illness don't want to get help is because they are scared. They are scared to admit they need help. They are also scared of the illness, as well as the possible treatment. The sufferer must want to be helped, but they are not in the best frame of mind to make appropriate decisions. Many times they are only able to properly concentrate and successfully handle a few minutes at a time and are not able to handle looking toward a future that involves any type of treatment. Yet, in the case of drug abuse or alcoholism, there must be some kind of treatment to stop the use of the drug.

2. HELP THEM FIND, TAKE, AND CONTINUE TO TAKE THE PROPER MEDICATION(S).

JEAN-CLAUDE - For the bipolar sufferer, it's important to find the right medication to help smooth out moods. Jean-Claude Van Damme, after four divorces and being charged with spouse abuse, shared that once he started taking the correct medication the water moving back and forth all around him became as smooth as a lake. Each person is different, so what medication works for one might not work for another.

Once the right medication is found, it must be taken. The trouble with most people with bipolar disorder and/or schizophrenia is when they start to feel better and are on the road to lead a more normal life, they believe they no longer need their medication and stop taking it. Someone who has schizophrenia or a bipolar disorder must take the medication and take it regularly.

> **In ugly times I picture blue;**
> **The sea, the sky, but mostly you**
> **The water helps to calm my mind,**
> **The heavens heal my heart.**
> **My soul is left, and it is yours,**
> **My being rests with you.**
> **When all is dark and I can't see**
> **It helps to picture blue.**
> **~~~Stone Ronson**

MARIETTE - When actress Mariette Hartley finally got her bipolar condition under control after being misdiagnosed with depression and ADD, she warned others to stay on the right medication. She also encouraged them to keep searching for the correct medication if their current medication was unsuccessful.

VIRGINIA AND VIVIEN - Writer Virginia Woolf committed suicide after psychiatry alone seemed to have no effect on her mental condition. Actor Vivien Leigh ruined her professional reputation and marriage to Lawrence Olivier because the right medication and clinics were not available to her. She would swing between being happy and being miserable. She thought her problem consisted solely of her impatient and headstrong qualities, which she erroneously and continually believed she could control.

SINEAD - Singer Sinead O'Connor had said before she was diagnosed correctly every one of the pores of her body cried, and she didn't know why or what for. She feels she died and was born again after taking the correct medications and taking them properly.

3. GIVE SUPPORT AS A FRIEND OR FAMILY MEMBER, BUT DON'T ENABLE THEM.

It's important to know where to go to get help for a friend or family member. NAMI (National Alliance on Mental Illness) is a good organization that can give advice on how to help you, as well as the sufferer of mental illness. Their website is **www.nami.org** and their helpline is 800.950.NAMI.

It's also important your support and love be unconditional. Make sure, though, you know the difference between enablement and unconditional support. When you enable someone, you help them avoid consequences of their bad behavior, which in turn helps them to continue to make poor choices. You can always love someone and wish the best for them without lying or making excuses for them. Showing unconditional love does not mean you have to fund their mess-ups with your hard-earned money. Unconditional love and acceptance means you realize you can't "fix" them. You can help, support, or inspire. You can be there for them when they are willing to help themselves, but you have to be able to take up for yourself.

SLASH - Slash, former Guns N' Roses guitarist, was diagnosed with congestive heart failure because of his extensive alcohol and heroin use. His wife helped him give up his addictions, but she didn't "fix" him. He made the decision to do what it took to quit.

MATT AND BEN - Matt Damon smoked cigarettes for 17 years and worked his way up to a pack and a half a day. He gave up smoking to improve his chances of having children and was inspired by his brother who had kicked the habit. Damon was then in a position to help his good friend, Ben Affleck, to also kick the habit when Ben's daughter Violet was born.

ROBERT - Actor Robert Downey, Jr. had been a drug addict since he was eight years old and was forced time and time again into rehab which did little to encourage him to clean up. Downey's wife, producer Susan Levin, is credited to have helped turn him around. She said she would not marry him until he kicked his drug habit, which he did. When Downey gave up his addictions, he said he felt like he had come out of a 20-year coma. He went from the poster boy for wasted talent to sign the first $100 million movie contract in history for two movies in the Iron Man series.

4. HELP THEM FIND SOMETHING TO FILL THE VOID.

CARRIE, BRITNEY, AND ERIC - Something must fill the void the illness occupied in the victim's life. For instance, Carrie Fisher got her condition under control because she wanted to be a good mother. She is quoted as saying she stopped feeling, "It's my business if I wanted to stop my medication." She no longer feels that way. She understands it is also the business of those around her whom she affects. Britney Spears also went into rehab for alcohol and other drug abuse for her children. Singer Eric Clapton at one time paid $16,000 a day for his drug problem. Once he kicked the habit, he filled that void when he started a drug and alcohol addiction treatment center.

JENNIFER AND JON - Actress Jennifer Aniston uses Yoga and a healthy lifestyle to relax her so she doesn't smoke cigarettes again. Comedian/talk show host Jon Stewart keeps a gumball machine close by when he works to use a gumball to detour that desire for a cigarette.

BRIAN AND PATTY - Brian "Head" Welch, co-founder of the metal band Korn, said what helped him the most was to become a Christian. Since his conversion, he's dedicated his life to helping others. Actress Patty Duke had attempted suicide five times before her mental illness was properly diagnosed and treated. She became the first celebrity to publically share her struggles and work hard to educate the public on mental illness issues.

5. SUGGEST THEY SEEK PROFESSIONAL HELP AND ADVICE.

Leave the diagnoses and counseling to the professionals. If at first your family member or friend is reluctant to talk to a professional, encourage them to take a few of the online Mental Health assessment tests. Maybe after they see the results of these assessments, they will be more willing to set up an appointment with a professional.

EMOTIONAL HEALTH

Have you ever been bothered by noisy children at a movie? Were you able to control your annoyances and anger?

A father took his children to a south Philadelphia showing of *The Curious Case of Benjamin Button* one Christmas night. Because the children were noisy, a nearby moviegoer got upset, threw popcorn at the son, and took out a firearm and shot the father. The shooter most definitely did not show proper Emotional Intelligence.

There are people who believe showing any kind of emotion is bad. What do you think? Would it be a better world if no one showed emotions? There was a man who had bad headaches caused by a tumor the size of an orange. When the tumor was removed, doctors also removed some connecting tissue. The tumor was not malignant, and at first everything seemed fine for the man. But all was not well. The surgery not only removed the tumor; it removed his emotions.

He no longer experienced emotions such as anger, frustrations, sadness, or grief. He lost his job, got divorced, remarried, and divorced again. Having no emotions wrecked his marriages and his life.

> **Anyone can become angry - that is easy, but to be angry with the right person at the right time, and for the right purpose and in the right way - that is not within everyone's power and that is not easy.**
> **~~~Aristotle**

The animated movie, *Inside Out*, demonstrated how our emotions, like joy, sadness, anger, disgust, and fear are all important and needed. But if they are missing, or used in the wrong manner, we become out of sync. The movie's director, screenwriter, and developer, Pete Docter, got the idea for the movie when he witnessed his own daughter going through emotional changes as she got older.

Since we need our emotions, we have to use intelligence to help use them properly. That is why the term "Emotional Intelligence" or EI has been such a buzzword since the early 1990s.

Do you know and understand your feelings? Do you possess the skills to use your feelings to make proper decisions? If not, you might want to work on your Emotional Intelligence.

When I googled the words "Emotional Intelligence," my computer screen showed almost 27 million results. I saw such headlines as "EI--Why it is, and Why it Matters," and "EI--Why it Can Matter More Than IQ." When I saw "Caffeine--the Silent Killer of Emotional Intelligence," I put down my half-drunk can of Coke Zero to find out, according to *Forbes Magazine*, caffeine was depriving my brain of the oxygen I needed to keep me calm and rational. There were advertisements for books on EI, as well as invitations to attend workshops.

I even saw where you could take an EI test to find out what your EI was and how to improve it. One article promised EI was important for leadership, another announced it is the foundation for critical skills, and yet another told me to look at pictures of faces to guess which emotions were conveyed to make me more EI savvy. I was wooed to look at websites with free articles and books to teach me everything I ever wanted to know about EI, but I couldn't find them. Instead, I found books I could purchase at a low, low price to improve my EI. I was mildly depressed to find even though I was born with a huge amount of brain cells, I will steadily lose them until I die unless I buy some guy's book. Reading his book and turning his suggestions into actions would save my brain cells and give me 360-degree feedback on EI competencies.

There is a debate in psychology whether EI is simply a genetic characteristic or if it can be learned. I feel the Nature vs. Nurture debate will continue, but what I do know is EI centers on abilities to **understand, control, and correctly evaluate** our emotions.

I challenge you to psychologically acquire help in understanding, controlling and correctly evaluating your emotions. This growth will require you to rethink and restructure Your Professional, Personal, and Financial Life, but the payoff is you can get off The Low Road and get on the path leading to The High Road. The higher your level of Emotional Intelligence, the sooner you make it to The High Road, and the better the chance you will stay there.

When I worked for a governmental agency which helped individuals with a disability or multiple disabilities to keep or be able to get a job, a client shared she wanted the agency to pay for an additional educational degree. She already had one degree and was not able to keep a job in the education field. She felt another degree in another area would help her to get a job and keep it. After I had talked with her for a few minutes, I realized her physical disability didn't keep her from being able to hold on to a job. It was her level of Emotional Intelligence. She did not know how to react to situations and individuals in her work environment in the proper manner.

We can be illiterate in our emotions much the same as we can be illiterate in our ability to read and comprehend the written word. Can you control your emotions? Do you feel the need to constantly confront those around you? Do uncontrollable displays of your emotions affect your Professional and Personal Life in a negative way?

If you answer yes to any of those questions, you may need an Emotional Intelligence boost.

The following four attributes can work together to give you an Emotional Intelligence boost.

1. SELF-AWARENESS.

Know your strengths and weaknesses and how your emotions affect you and your behavior.

2. SELF-MANAGEMENT.

Once you know how your emotions affect you and your behavior, learn to control those emotions, especially the very impulsive ones, in a positive and healthy way through self-control and adapting to changing and diverse environments.

3. SOCIAL-AWARENESS.

Once you understand your own emotions and can control them, then you can become aware of the emotions of others and be able to adjust yours to theirs which can help you adapt socially.

4. RELATIONSHIP-MANAGEMENT.

After conquering the first three parts of Emotional Intelligence, you are able to build relationships, maintain them, manage conflict, and even possibly influence and inspire those around you to join you on The High Road.

If you can't master those four attributes of Emotional Intelligence, you may want to evaluate your stress level. Stress can overwhelm you and take over your ability to read a situation accurately.

CAROLYN - Trust your gut instinct. There is a reality in the expression, follow your gut, as there are cells in your stomach that in times of stress signal to your brain to get busy doing something about the stress. These cells are stomach bacteria called, "gut flora." For more information, look up the July 2, 2011, issue of *Psychology Today*. Carolyn C. Ross, MD, discusses how gut flora communicates with our brain cells to help us combat Mental and Physical Health conditions. She says stress can cause gut flora to change or get out of balance. This new condition is signaled to the brain, and the brain then takes steps to do what is needed to help combat that stress.

I would also recommend using humor in a constructive manner. A good hearty laugh brings our nervous system back into balance. Humor shows maturity and can diffuse a volatile situation. It can help you be a better leader, because when you can make someone laugh, you can make someone listen.

A Robert Half International survey showed 84% of executives polled thought people do a better job if they have a sense of humor, and a whopping 91% thought a good sense of humor is important for career advancement. Humor shows you can see the forest despite the trees, but it can be hard to do well, and is easy to do badly. In fact, depending on the situation, the time, and who you're telling a joke about or to, it can even be deadly. Back in Nazi Germany times, a factory worker named Marianne was arrested and executed when she told a version of the following joke.

Adolph Hitler and Luftwaffe-Chief Herman Goring were standing on top of the Berlin radio tower. Hitler asked Goring, "Can you think of anything I could do that would cheer up the people of Berlin?" Chief Goring responded quickly by saying, "Jump."

It didn't matter Hitler was considered a jokester and had ridiculed and make fun of Chief Goring. Hitler even told jokes that often disturbed those around him. A telephonist and bodyguard in the Berlin Bunker where Adolph Hitler spent the last days of his life, named Rochus Misch, wrote a book called, *Hitler's Last Witness*. In this book, Misch shared how many of Hitler's jokes were about concentration camp victims.

FRANKLIN, JOHN, AND MARINA - It's also important to learn good Conflict Management skills when driving down The High Road. E. Franklin Dukes, John B. Stephens, and Marina A. Piscolish, in their book, *Reaching for Higher Ground in Conflict Resolution*, refer to the higher ground as being "a place where behavior is expected and rewarded." They say The High Road is where "truth telling and truth seeking are honored, where integrity is valued, and where trust is given because trust is earned." They stress how Conflict Resolution is more than reaching common ground. Knowing and using some of the basic skills of Conflict Management can definitely improve your EI.

I believe you can use these 5 A's (Acknowledge, Analyze, Assess, Alter, and Action) in your approach to deal with conflict.

1. ACKNOWLEDGE THE CONFLICT.

An ostrich with its head in the sand is not attractive and neither are you if you stand around with your head in the sand and your butt in the air. When you acknowledge there is a conflict, it is the first step to deal with a conflict. This doesn't mean you have to admit you're wrong or have done something wrong. Actually, many conflicts are based on differences in perception where there does not have to be a wrong party. I'm sure we all understand the half full/half empty glass differences in perception. If I say the glass is half full, I am right. If you say it's half empty, you are right. It's a matter of perception. We may have conflict over this issue until we acknowledge the conflict and realize it may simply be a difference in perception, and we are both right.

2. ANALYZE THE CONFLICT.

Is this conflict something you can control? Some things are within our control, but some things aren't. Learn the Serenity Prayer. Especially that part about how we should accept things we can't change. The only thing worse than standing around with your head in the sand and your butt in the air when you have conflict is spinning your wheels in the sand going nowhere because you have no control over a situation. After you analyze a conflict and realize you have no control, you have to let it go. To continue to spin your wheels in the sand only gets sand all over you and those around you, which leads to frustration and resentment.

3. ASSESS YOUR CONTRIBUTION TO THE CONFLICT.

Ask the question, "What part did I play in this conflict?" Honest and open communication is extremely important. What did you bring to the conflict? Did you apply gasoline to the fire, or did you try to put out the fire? Did you intentionally push someone's buttons? Have you allowed the other party or parties to express their side? When you open up to listen to the other side with all emotions involved (without an interruption or interjection of your own opinions) you set the stage for the conflict to be resolved. This also makes it easier for the other party to listen to your concerns.

4. ALTER THE PERCEPTIONS.

After hearing the other side of the conflict, it may take some soul searching to decide to turn the conflicts and perceptions from negative to positive. When you start to understand the other points of view, do you let go of your resentments and perceptions? Was the conflict based on not enough, or improper, respect? Was it simply a difference of opinion? If so, alter your feelings to allow diversity. We should all learn to get along with those who are different or think differently. Don't have a victim mentality. If you do, shake it off. When someone has a different opinion than yours, it doesn't mean you are being degraded or humiliated. Alter your perceptions.

5. TAKE **ACTION.**

After accomplishing the first 4 A's, take action. Our brains were created to make a connection with other humans. Some U.S. soldiers went to a mosque to ask a leader a question. The leader didn't trust the soldiers and was afraid the Americans would either destroy the mosque or try to arrest him, so he had his soldiers quickly surround the American soldiers. The American commander ordered his troops to point their rifles downward, get on their knees, smile, and very slowly move backward as they continued to smile. Soon the American soldiers' actions were copied, and a volatile situation was averted. We are designed to be sociable, even in a routine encounter, according to Daniel Goleman, an authority on Emotional, Social, and Ecological Intelligence.

PHYSICAL HEALTH

We are often bombarded with advertisements which tell us to lose weight and exercise more to improve Our Physical Health, but experts can't agree on the correct ways to accomplish that. A tactic considered helpful one day is considered useless on another.

Some Dos and Don'ts to help you maintain Superior Physical Health are

- ✓ **Do eat sensibly**
- ✓ **Do get enough rest**
- ✓ **Do smile and laugh often**

- ✓ **Don't take yourself or your life too seriously**
- ✓ **Don't drink alcoholic beverages to excess**
- ✓ **Don't work too hard**
- ✓ **Don't smoke**

An excellent resource for advice on Physical Health issues is the Mayo Clinic website. When I perused this website, I found seven benefits to being involved in regular physical activity which are: **controls weight, combats health conditions and diseases, improves mood, boosts energy, promotes better sleep, puts the spark back into a sex life, and it is fun.** I also read we should aim for at least 30 minutes of physical activity every day. If we want to lose weight, we will have to exercise more. The site recommended checking with your doctor before you start any new exercise program, especially if you have any chronic health problems such as heart disease or diabetes.

FRANCOIS - Francois de La Rochefoucauld wrote when a reader reads his maxims (proverbs) the reader should put it in the mind right from the start that none of the maxims apply in particular. The reader should also think he/she is the sole exception, even though the maxims appear to be in generalities. We may not have to be educated on how important it is to take care of Our Physical Health, but occasionally we have to be reminded. La Rochefoucauld also said, "To eat is a necessity, but to eat intelligently is an art." This is an especially interesting proverb as he was unable to abide by it and died of gout in Paris on March 17, 1680.

A good laugh and a long sleep are the best cures in the doctor's book. ~~~An Irish Proverb

Eat sensibly, and get some exercise a few times a week to keep up Your Physical Health. As my brother Ros has often told me, "If you want to lose weight and feel better, you have to move more and eat less."

SPIRITUAL HEALTH

Good Spiritual Health means your mind, body, and soul all have a good connection with each other.

I recommend these six things to improve your Spiritual Life.

1. HAVE A MEANINGFUL RELATIONSHIP WITH GOD, AS WELL AS YOUR LOVED ONES.

I do believe it's important to have a meaningful relationship with God. I also believe it's important to have meaningful relationships with your loved ones. Identify those you care about and work hard at those relationships to make them good ones. Positive, meaningful relationships will improve your connection with your mind, body, and soul. I often call my youngest brother John because I know before we end the call, he will tell me at least two times he loves me. Having positive, meaningful relationships with those you care about can boost Your Spiritual Health while dysfunctional relationships break down Your Spiritual Health.

In the movie, *The River Runs Through It*, a minister and father of two sons tells his congregation how we often see our loved ones in need and want to help, but we can seldom help those closest to us. This happens because we don't know what part of ourselves to give, or we feel what we have to give won't be wanted. He then makes a powerful point. He says it is possible to *love completely* without *complete understanding*.

We do not have to completely understand our loved ones to accept and love them completely. When we try to pick and choose which parts of our loved ones we will love and accept, our own Spiritual Health is affected in a negative way.

2. ATTEND RELIGIOUS SERVICES.

Find a group of people you relate to and who relate to you. One of the best reasons to affiliate with a religious group is to increase the opportunities for you to be of service and to help others in your city, state, country, and the world. This can help you stay on The High Road and be put in a position to help others find The High Road. Many studies show people who are religious report greater feelings of wellbeing than those who do not consider themselves religious. Religious individuals tend to be more positive, healthier and live longer.

3. SPEND DAILY TIME IN MEDITATION OR PRAYER.

Meditation and prayer can smooth out your rough edges, make those potholes of life seem smaller, and give you peace.

4. LOOK FOR AND FIND INSPIRATION.

You can find inspiration in a variety of places. It can be through reading, listening to music, and getting to know the stories of individuals who have overcome pain, suffering, poverty, and other obstacles.

5. FORGIVE, FORGET, AND GET ON WITH YOUR LIFE.

Not being able to forgive and/or forget breaks YOUR spirit. Be able to let go of past wrongs against you. Your soul is refreshed to be free of hate and vengeance. It's been said that 70% of the people we come in contact with each day are angry about something. Let's not be one of those angry people. Forgive, forget, and get on with your life. After all, you can't unscramble eggs.

JUNE - June Steenkamp has been able to forgive Oscar Pistorius, at least intellectually, for killing her only child, Reeva. She doesn't believe everything that happened the night Reeva was killed came out in the trial, and I'm sure she would like to have Oscar tell her more than what was released. It was important for her to forgive him for her own sake and because she's a Christian. She chose not to live with bitterness or allow bitterness into her heart. Instead, June is trying to do something positive by setting up a trust fund in Reeva's name to establish shelters for abused women.

Flying out of Des Moines, Iowa, to Denver, Colorado, one gloomy afternoon in April, I was struck by how brightly the sun shone as we rose above storm clouds. It's sad some people never seem to be able to rise above their storm clouds to see the sunshine.

I believe June is trying to rise above her storm clouds to find her sunshine. She feels a strong calling to relay important information about violence against women, especially in South Africa.

Even though June has forgiven Oscar, she still has to go on with her life. How easy is it to get on with your life when someone has done you wrong? Could you have forgiven the man who killed your only daughter? Could you really let it go? What if the actions of someone put you in prison for five years and probation for five more for a crime you didn't commit?

BRIAN - I saw a televised interview Ann Curry conducted with a 26-year-old man named Brian Banks. Brian had been exonerated from a crime he never committed after ten grueling years which included five years in prison, five years of probation, being labeled a sex offender, and the wearing of an ankle monitor, before his accuser finally stepped forward to admit the rape never happened.

When asked if his accuser should face prosecution, Brian replied he hadn't given it much thought. Ms. Curry continued to probe Brian's state of mind by asking if he wanted revenge. Brian showed his class and took The High Road when he acknowledged he'd had moments when he was angry and vengeful but knew it was best to move forward in a positive way for his own betterment.

Brian refused to let what happened to him affect his spirit. What do you need to let go of and move away from for the sake of your spirit? Remember it's for your own betterment and not for the one or ones who did something to you. In fact, it's highly possible they haven't given it, OR YOU, much thought at all.

6. SEEK OUT AND INCORPORATE PROPER COPING SKILLS.

Stress can wreck Your Spiritual Health if you can't find appropriate ways to cope. Drinking, smoking, overeating, and promiscuity are not good solutions; try walking, playing tennis, meditating, attending counseling, or confiding in a friend you can trust.

In trying to cope with situations, do not worry or use negative self-talk. Mrs. Blyss Weatherford, one of my high school teachers, once told me, "Worry is having mental pictures of what you don't want to happen." Her statement has stuck with me and helped me not to worry so much.

Another way to cope is to be willing to accept help from others. Have you heard the story of the man trapped in his house during a flood who prayed to God to save him?

A neighbor came by in a canoe and asked the man if he needed any help. The man said, "No, but thank you. I'm waiting on God to save me." The water kept rising, and soon the man had to go upstairs to his bedroom. A group came by in a speedboat and offered the man a ride to safety. The man said, "No, but thank you. I'm waiting on God to save me." The water kept rising, and soon the man was on top of his house. A helicopter flew over, and down came a ladder. A voice from above told the man to climb up the ladder to safety. He turned down the offer and said, "No, but thank you. I'm waiting on God to save me." The man eventually drowned. When he met God he said, "God, I prayed for you to save me. What happened?" God smiled and replied, "I sent two boats and a helicopter. What else did you expect me to do?" This man should have accepted the help of the people God put in the man's life. Do you accept the help of those God puts in your life?

REINHOLD - Rely on the Serenity Prayer to help you with stressful situations. I have the serenity prayer in several locations so when I experience stress I can read the words, "God grant me the serenity to accept the things I cannot change; courage to change the things I can; and wisdom to know the difference."

The words of this prayer were attributed to a man named Reinhold Niebuhr who was born in Wright City, Missouri. He won the Presidential Medal of Freedom. His writings have had a positive effect on such political leaders as Barack Obama, Jimmy Carter, Martin Luther King, Jr., Hillary Rodham Clinton, Hubert Humphrey, Dean Acheson, Madeleine Albright, and John McCain. Learn to dismiss from your mind what you have no control over.

Good luck with getting Your Mental, Emotional, Physical, and Spiritual elements of Your High Road in sync. You can do this by keeping your motor tuned and your tires balanced.

***

*COMMENTS AND NOTES ON
HOW TO KEEP YOUR MOTOR TUNED AND TIRES
BALANCED.*

_____

_____

_____

CHAPTER FIVE - BEWARE OF PESKY POTHOLES
(DON'T GET DISCOURAGED)

TOM - The winter of 2014 was an unusually brutal winter all over the United States, setting new record low temperatures coupled with record amounts of snow. One March 2014 morning, I watched a TV news story where Reporter Tom Costello, commented how three-fourths of cities and states by the end of February had already outspent their winter maintenance budgets.

He also said many state and city officials were calling special news conferences to talk about potholes and how the former Secretary of Transportation had said Congress needed to supply billions of dollars of repair money. Costello even gave statistics on how expensive it was to fix the damage potholes did to axles, struts, control arms, steering mechanisms, tire rims and tires, and how he had sustained almost $900 of pothole damage to his vehicle.

After listening to Mr. Costello's report, I thought about how potholes can also wreak havoc on your car and your journey on The High Road. This intrigued me to research potholes and their repair.

After further research, I found out Jimmy Fallon had said there were so many potholes in New York City that they were like the craters on the moon. I also found out there are two things that must be present to make a pothole--water and traffic. Undoubtedly, Jimmy Fallon, New York City must have a lot of both those elements.

I started to feel like a civil engineer as I read how roads are surfaced with layers. (Up to that point the closest I had ever gotten to civil engineering was to have dated a guy who was majoring in the field.)

When roads are paved, workers start with a foundation of soil (with rocks for drainage) and end with a layer of asphalt (a sticky concoction of hydrocarbons and gravel mixed with petroleum byproducts) on top. The stress of traffic creates cracks and holes in the asphalt. Water seeps down into the underlying soil/gravel foundation and freezes, which then expands and pushes out some of the dirt and gravel creating even larger cracks and holes. (*Are you bored yet?*)

Most damage to roads is cumulative so it's very important to have a plan to patch the potholes. In some cities, it's said they have two seasons--winter and pothole repair. During the cold weather, a throw-and-roll approach is used to fill up the pothole, and a big heavy vehicle compacts the asphalt down. When it's warm enough, a semi-permanent method is used where the water and debris is taken out before the roads are resurfaced resulting in the use of more labor, more equipment, and more time than the throw-and-roll method.

I once visited Winnipeg, in the Canadian Province of Manitoba, in August. Our tour of the city was constantly interrupted by crews resurfacing and refurbishing the roads. The tour guide mentioned these crews start work as soon as the weather gets warm enough and don't stop until the first blizzard.

If potholes aren't maintained, expensive damage can be done to a car's suspension and tires. In our High Road journey, we can also have expensive damage done to our dreams and ambitions.

 **HIGH ROAD HINT #6 – TURN POTHOLES INTO STEPPING STONES TO GET YOU TO WHERE YOU NEED TO GO.**

People often call events and individuals who get in their way of accomplishing goals, stumbling blocks. Whether you call them stumbling blocks or potholes, you have to see them for what they are. Sometimes they make you feel like a failure and tell you to give up on your dreams or goals. When those pesky potholes appear, you have to take action and turn them into stepping stones to get you to where you need to go.

There are three things that can make potholes appear more often or increase their intensity. They are insufficient thickness of pavement, bad drainage, and improper or lack of maintenance. In the next chapter (Chapter Six) we will learn how we need to pave our road with the proper materials (Respect, Rules, Resourcefulness, and Responsibility). These materials will give you thick pavement to help you stay true to your commitment to staying on The High Road no matter how many potholes get in your way. When you are wrongfully criticized, you have to get out your umbrella so those raindrops of criticism drain right off and don't fall on you. When you are discouraged, repair Your Mental, Emotional, Physical, and Spiritual Health. Potholes and keep on trucking.

KARL - A business executive named Karl Wadensten took action to make Rhode Island the first state to be free of potholes. He offered to donate a small vibratory roller that could be pushed like a lawnmower to every Rhode Island municipality. This machine could be used in the winter and did a semi-permanent job instead of the throw and roll-method. Fourteen municipalities had taken him up on his deal by March 12, 2014.

DAVIDE AND CLAUDIA - Davide Luciano, a photographer, and Claudia Ficca, a food stylist, bring attention to potholes located in cities like New York City, Los Angeles, Montreal, and Toronto. They stage and photograph them and then post the photos online. One online photo had a man stomping grapes in a pothole, another showed people with their dogs standing in line watching a lady washing her dog in a pothole. All the pictures include actual potholes in actual cities portrayed in very unique and creative photographs.

A long, long time ago there was a king who placed an enormous boulder in the middle of a busy road. He then hid to see if anyone would move it. Over and over again he observed wealthy and intelligent merchants walking around the boulder without trying to move it. The king could even hear some of them noisily blaming their king for doing such a poor job of keeping the roadway clear. Then a lowly peasant came along carrying his heavy load of vegetables. When he saw the boulder, he laid down his vegetables and pushed and pushed until he moved it out of the way. The peasant immediately saw a purse lying in the roadway where the boulder used to be. Inside were several gold coins and a note from the king saying the person or persons moving the boulder could keep the coins as a reward. The peasant learned a valuable lesson that day, which was the boulder contained an opportunity to improve his present condition. Potholes and obstacles may contain opportunities to improve your present condition.

GILBERT - Gilbert Tuhabonye knows all about pesky potholes and obstacles. Throughout his life, he has used them to improve his condition and help others. In 1974, Gilbert was born in southern Burundi, a small, mountainous country located in east-central Africa. Gilbert's parents were farmers and part of the Tutsi tribe, raising potatoes, peas, corn, and beans. Gilbert developed a desire to run, running five miles to and from school each day while he raced friends and sometimes even the family cows.

After completing the sixth grade, Gilbert was sent to board at a Protestant school in Kibimba, 150 miles away. He showed his speed immediately, winning an 8K race barefoot in the ninth grade. His running technique was strengthened by a mentor and coach who encouraged him to reach for the stars and train for the Olympics. In the eleventh grade, his hard work was rewarded when Gilbert became the national champion in the 400 and 800 meters. By his senior year in high school, Gilbert was on The High Road determined to receive a scholarship to an American school and obtain a college education.

But life doesn't always turn out how you expect it to. Sometimes you can run into a few potholes. One day in October 1993, the brutality between the Tutsi and Hutu tribes erupted and the Hutu tribe members overtook his Kibimba school. Fellow classmates, along with parents and some school faculty, barricaded Gilbert and other classmates and teachers from the Tutsi tribe. Gilbert and his fellow Tutsi tribe members were beaten and set on fire. In flames, Gilbert was forced to bury himself under the bones and corpses of his friends and teachers.

After nine long hours, Gilbert escaped from the burning building by using a charred bone to break a window. Gilbert ran and ran and ran from this scene toward the nearest hospital. As he lay in the hospital, the only surviving Tutsi member of his school, he couldn't understand why the people who were his teachers and friends had tried to murder him.

He began running after a painful healing period, even though doctors had informed him he would never run again. Gilbert didn't allow the potholes to deter him from achieving his goal to receive an American education; he attended The University of Georgia on a track scholarship. He was recruited by Abilene Christian University where he transferred and went on to earn All-American honors six times. In the 1996 Summer Olympics, he was one of the individuals who carried the Olympic torch, his leg of the journey being in Birmingham, Alabama. In 1999, he competed and proved to be the champion at the Lonestar Conference in both the 1500 meters and 8K Cross Country. Gilbert graduated from Abilene Christian and, despite the scar tissue from his extensive burns, became a national champion runner.

Gilbert hit another pothole in London trying to qualify for the Olympics. In an online blog entry, Gilbert gave insight to athletes answering the question, "How do I get over a bad race?" He simply said to learn from every race--what was done well, and what could have been done differently or better.

While running the London Marathon, Gilbert injured his hamstring, which ruined his chance to run in the Olympics. Even though he experienced another pothole, he gave tips to world-class athletes as they were preparing to journey to Beijing, China, for the 2008 Summer Olympic Games. He shared with them the wisdom learned from his own trials in London. Even in the most deplorable and trying times of his life, Gilbert Tuhabonye overcame the potholes to strive to help others on The High Road in spite of his harrowing past and own bad races. Gilbert later became a head cross country and track coach in Austin, Texas. He established a training program, Gilbert's Gazelles, through which he trained all levels of runners on how to run their best while limiting injuries. One of the runners he coached in his Gilbert's Gazelles Program named Patrick Guy said Gilbert was the most inspirational guy he ever met.

He also helped provide clean water to people in his homeland of Burundi, Africa. By April 2012, more than 11,000 had been helped. Even though he didn't win a medal in the Olympics, he is a champion and a success as an author and motivational speaker inspiring people all over the world with his life story. Through all the potholes of his life he says he ran as a carefree child through the mountains of Burundi, then he ran for his life, and now he runs for joy.

We should never believe once we get on The High Road there will never be any obstacles or potholes. Life is still life. Things happen. We have to learn to take the bad with the good. Some even believe having trials and tribulations make us stronger.

MIKO - One morning I watched my daughter's dog (Miko) eat a type of dog food called *Kibbles and Bits*. Miko made a concerted effort to ignore the Kibbles (the drab, harder, but more substantial morsels of the dog food) and only eat the Bits (the tastier, softer more colorful morsels). If by accident she did get a Kibbles in her mouth, she very politely positioned it on the floor around her food bowl to continue her search for more Bits.

It made me wonder if as a society we've become more of a Bits type of people. Do we look for the easier way out? Do we expect to have few, if any, hard experiences in life? Do we believe life owes us only soft, colorful, and tasty moments? Do we work hard to ignore the Kibbles? Do we strategically place Kibbles outside and around our bowl of life to consume tomorrow in the hopes tomorrow will never, ever present itself, even if *we bet our bottom dollar and the sun comes out."* (Sorry . . . I admit—I do so love the music and lyrics of the movie and musical, *Annie*.)

Through the music we listen to and the avenues of social media we read, we are constantly bombarded with lyrics and posts asking for and applauding those gifts of Bits. When Kibbles come along, there's groaning and moaning, and yes, quite a bit of drama, expressing indignation and disappointment. If we pray at all, do we pray to God to make our lives easy? Do we want lots and lots of material blessings and fun without desiring to work for them? Do we refuse to take on any Kibbles by putting effort into a relationship, whether it's to keep one or to cultivate one we already have?

We want Bits type of jobs or careers; forget those jobs containing Kibbles. We want to receive Bits remuneration and Bits types of success. If Kibbles should be completed, well, that's not our problem, let someone else tackle it. Kibbles are too hard. Chewing and eating Kibbles takes strong teeth and we don't want to take the chance one of our glossy whites could possibly be chipped.

Have we become a wimpy, self-serving lot? If so, let's get back to tackling Kibbles, perhaps even searching for them. Give me a K--Give me an I--Give me a B--Give me another B--Give me an L--Give me an E--Give me an S--What does that spell? KIBBLES ! ! ! Say it again.

KIBBLES ! ! ! What do we need to ask for and attack? KIBBLES ! ! ! (Sorry the ex-cheerleader in me for a minute raised her ugly head.)

Yes, indeed, let's confront and gobble up all those Kibbles in our lives. Let's ask for more to chomp down on. After all, we need stronger teeth and finely-toned, svelte bodies. Forget those silly Bits out there waiting to rot our teeth and make us weak and flabby. Let's look down on those who push aside their Kibbles and let them know how much healthier and better we are than they.

As I mused about the possibility of a utopian world full of tough, salubrious, no-nonsense Kibbles handlers, I suddenly realized that's not ideal either. I wouldn't want to live in that kind of world. I pondered if I knew any Kibbles only people. I soon realized I did. They were those who only looked for the negative. They liked their lives to be hard and yours as well. They looked down their noses at everyone who didn't believe or act as they did. I remembered how in the last several years so many Kibbles people ended up in politics and made the passage of even a simple piece of legislation that benefited everyone in our country, difficult, if not impossible.

Wow. What a novel and epiphany moment. My epiphany explained how we need the Kibbles, AND we need the Bits. The Bits help us to enjoy and savor our lives. Sometimes we need to let go. Sometimes we need to have some fun. Bits in our lives keep us young at heart and make it enjoyable for others to be around us and put up with us.

We also need Kibbles, because when we handle the Kibbles that come our way, we become stronger and our confidence increases. It's like the butterfly that eats what's inside her cocoon and then flaps her wings over and over again to break out. By attacking the Kibbles on the inside of her cocoon, she becomes tough enough to fly away with strong, viral wings to soar and savor the joy and beauty of her life.

As I now see the need for both Kibbles AND Bits, I am reminded of the perfect southern biscuit. (Yes. The perfect biscuit is a southern biscuit.) It's brown and a little crunchy on the outside, with the right amount of soft, fluffy center on the inside. The crunchy brown part allows me to break the biscuit open and smear a generous portion of butter and jam on each half without dropping a single crumb. The soft portion soaks up the butter and jam and holds the warmth until I pop a heavenly piece in my mouth.

So, God, forgive me when I ask for a Bits only life. Forgive me when I complain about the Kibbles that have come my way, upon honest reflection, made me stronger and more resilient. Please continue to give me a Kibbles AND Bits sort of life. Help me to Take The High Road and stay on The High Road by enjoying and sharing my Bits and attack with poise and determination the Kibbles I find on the road ahead.

And yes, after writing this, I did make some perfect, southern biscuits that I easily broke open. I smeared them, while still warm, with the right combination of butter and jam. Yum. Yum. I did not drop a single delicious crumb. Oh, the joy of a life filled with Kibbles AND Bits.

* * *

COMMENTS AND NOTES ON
HOW TO WATCH OUT FOR PESKY POTHOLES AND
NOT GET DISCOURAGED.

_____

_____

_____

Part Two –
Take The High Road
In Your Professional Life

<u>Chapter Six</u> - Pave Your Road with Proper Materials: Respect, Rules, Resourcefulness, and Responsibility, Page 71.

<u>Chapter Seven</u> - If You're Leading the Caravan, Make Sure Your GPS is Working (Be a Good Leader), Page 81.

<u>Chapter Eight</u> - Beware of Skunks, Deer, and Sunday Drivers (AKA Gossips, Bullies, and Goof-Offs), Page 85.

CHAPTER SIX - PAVE YOUR ROAD WITH PROPER MATERIALS: RESPECT, RULES, RESOURCEFULNESS, AND RESPONSIBILITY

As a manager and supervisor, I had four cornerstones I used to help me stay on My Professional High Road. I also encouraged subordinates to use those cornerstones as well. I called them legal/ethical, attendance, respect, and production. I would draw a square and put each of the four on a side and say these four are the four cornerstones of Our Professional Relationship. I then said, "As long as you do what you're supposed to do in each of these areas, I will not bother you. I will allow you to do your job."

FIGURE 2
AUSTIN'S 4 R'S OF
THE HIGH ROAD

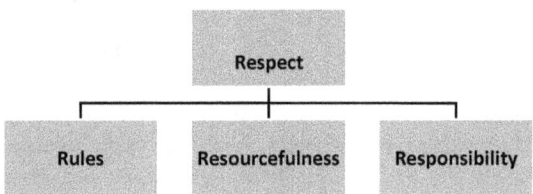

The only problem is I would remember the concepts but would forget what I actually labeled each corner. So I decided to make them all start with the same letter and in doing so, I have now revised them and call them, *Austin's 4 R's* of *The High Road.* They are *Respect, Rules, Resourcefulness, and Responsibility* as shown in **Figure 2.** I still have the 4 main ideas; I revised them so they're easier to remember.

On The High Road, I believe *Respect, Rules, Resourcefulness,* and *Responsibility* should be the materials you use to pave your road in Your Professional Life. So let's discuss each one in a little more detail.

RESPECT

Aretha Franklin has sung a popular song demanding RESPECT. Author and motivational speaker, John W. Gardner once said, "If you have some Respect for people as they are, you can be more effective in helping them to become better than they are."

Respect yourself, and others will Respect you.
~~~Confucius

It is important to show Respect in the workplace. First to yourself and then to others. I believe everyone deserves to be treated with respect, whether they are at the bottom of the organizational chart or at the top.

 **HIGH ROAD HINT #7 – PAVE YOUR HIGH ROAD WITH RESPECT, RULES, RESOURCEFULNESS, AND RESPONSIBILITY.**

PAUL - Paul Marciano, the grandson of the author/illustrator of the Madeline series of children books, is an organizational psychologist passionate about Respect. He believes personal and work relationships are successful only if they are in the context of Respect. Once that happens, employees are engaged. He stresses managers have to help employees Respect all elements and individuals of the organization.

Paul wrote the book, *Carrots and Sticks Don't Work: Build a Culture of Employee Engagement with the Principles of RESPECT*. The elements of his model are.

1. **Recognition**
2. **Empowerment**
3. **Supportive Feedback**
4. **Partnering**
5. **Expectations**
6. **Consideration**
7. **Trust**
8. **Respect**

I especially believe in the importance of his #6 and #7. Before any of his other drivers can be given, the foundation of consideration and trust must be established. Without them, the rest cannot be upheld.

You never know what lies ahead in the future. Sometimes the money is not there to give a raise or improve working conditions. Respect is one thing that does not cost money we can give to each other and managers and owners can give their employees.

RULES

Know Rules and follow them. They are necessary for a peaceful and orderly Professional, as well as Personal and Financial Life. Rules help keep us safe. Can you imagine what traffic would be like if there were no Rules governing when traffic should stop, and when it should go, when pedestrians should walk, and when they should remain still? Without Rules, others could take what you worked hard for, and you would have to let them.

IRENA - Irena Sendler knows what it's like to witness the actions of people who are not subject to Rules and are not accountable for their actions. She saw Jewish children murdered and sent to concentration camps by the Nazis. Irena and her team of 20 saved approximately 2,500 Jewish babies and children as they smuggled them out of Poland in ambulances and trams and gave them new identities between October 1940 and April 1943. Sometimes the babies and smaller children were wrapped up as packages. Irena had them placed with Polish families, orphanages, and Roman Catholic convents.

She wrote all their real names down on pieces of paper in the hopes they would someday be reunited with their families. When the Nazis arrested Irena, she had filled jars with the names and buried them in one of her assistant's yard. She was severely tortured and sentenced to death but was able to evade execution and survive the war.

"It took a true miracle to save a Jewish child," Elzbieta Ficowska, who was saved by Sendler's team as a baby in 1942, recalled in an AP interview in 2007. "Mrs. Sendler saved not only us but also our children and grandchildren and the generations to come."

Confined to a nursing home in her last years, Irena Sendler was finally acknowledged for her efforts. Poland's President, Lech Kaczynski and other politicians put together a campaign to nominate Irena for the Nobel Peace Prize.

She lived to be 98, and Kansas students produced a play based on her life called, *Life in a Jar*. This play has been performed all across the United States, Canada, and Poland sharing her story.

As employees, we should know the policies and Rules of our organizations and abide by them. If your company has a code of ethics, abide by it, and keep on hand the code of ethics for your profession. In Your Professional Life, as in Your Personal Life, it's important to understand and set your own boundaries as well as show Respect and acknowledge the boundaries set by others.

Boundaries help to define us. They help us to separate ourselves from others. They empower us and help others to understand how we want to be treated.

RESOURCEFULNESS

To even begin to pave Your High Road with Resourcefulness you have to have as a foundation the bare minimum, which is to know what is required of you for your job or career and do it. You must know where to go to obtain needed information. You must take care of resources you've been entrusted with, whether it's supplies, money, or people. Sometimes you may not have enough information, or maybe you find out you have the wrong information and/or materials, or there appears to be no plan. This puts you in a difficult situation. When this happens, you have to pave Your High Road with a layer of Resourcefulness.

Being Resourceful means you can break out of those difficult, unplanned situations by using your brain as well as what is readily available. You might even look around for common materials at hand, or in a nearby closet, and create a hot air balloon to escape Soviets; manipulate a fire hose with a Swiss army knife to make a zip-line to escape Mafia hit men; build a plane from a tent, the engine of a lawn mower, and a lot of duct tape; and take a scarf and a rock to make a slingshot to knock a bad guy off a horse with one swift flick of your wrist.

Are you hungry? Make a fishing lure from a gum wrapper and go fishing. Did your co-worker have a heart attack? Spring into action by using a floor mat, candlestick holders, and a power cord to assemble a defibrillator to bring him back to life and then take apart a bicycle and reconstruct it to fashion a cart to transport that co-worker to the hospital. Curious and need to listen in on an enemy landline telephone conversation? Use tweezers and a coat hanger to do the job. Find an old gramophone record with no sign of a gramophone? Take some paper and a safety pin and listen away.

Stumble across a skull and wonder who the person was? Take pencil erasers, cotton wool, and modeling clay and mold the face back on. Now you recognize that person. Trapped in a locked room wearing handcuffs? Search until you find a bobby pin to spring open the lock on your handcuffs and then use those same handcuffs to pick the lock of the door to escape.

If any of the previous scenarios sound somewhat familiar, you probably watched TV from 1985 – 1992 (or saw the reruns) and recognize these mind-boggling events being accomplished by a person of true Resourcefulness--Secret Agent Angus MacGyver. My personal favorite is when he uses his Swiss Army knife and a paper clip to disarm a nuclear missile with only one second to spare.

Even though MacGyver was a fictitious character starring in a fictitious television show, the term "MacGyverism" is used in the real world to represent being able to get out of a difficult situation with creativity and imagination, or as I call it, Resourcefulness.

One thing that can help you improve your creativity and imagination quotient is to associate with people who are more successful than you. Find mentors and be willing to take their advice. Spend time with them. Listen to their stories of how they used problem-solving skills to dissect and triumph over difficult dilemmas. Read and listen to the writings and experiences of famous Resourceful people and pave your High Road with Resourcefulness.

RESPONSIBILITY

To show you are responsible, you should be dependable, trustworthy, and accountable.

THOMAS, NELLIE, AND BOOKER - Examples of individuals we know who have shown elements of Responsibility are Thomas Jefferson, when he took on the Responsibility to be the main author of the Declaration of Independence; Nellie Bly who advocated women's rights and exposed the horrible conditions of orphans and prisoners; and Booker T. Washington who devoted most of his life to build up and promote Tuskegee Institute and celebrate and encourage civil rights for people of all races and colors.

While on a work/vacation trip to Hawaii, I talked to several individuals who spent almost every possible moment on the beach to surf the waves. At first I perceived them all to be irResponsible until my very interesting conversation with one surfer in particular. I started to stereotype him to be this "irResponsible surfer dude," because he surfed practically every morning the weather permitted. *After all*, I thought, *anyone who hangs around the beach all day (not on vacation) and does nothing but surf has to be a bum. I bet he never pays any taxes and always looks for a handout.*

Much to my surprise he was a very successful Oracle Programmer who had moved to Hawaii from Canada, and made a very lucrative salary. The reason I know about the "lucrative" part of that equation is because when I got back to the mainland and googled "Oracle Programmer positions," I saw how much more he was paid as I as a college professor with 30 years of experience had been. Since the majority of his work is done online, he is permitted to establish his own schedule and decide his own hours. He told me how he budgeted his time wisely to be able to have his alone time to surf.

As our conversation continued to progress, my first perception he was an irResponsible surfer dude changed to see the reality that he was a Responsible, tax-paying, hard-working employee, loyal husband, and loving father.

In the next few pages will be my thoughts about another "surfer dude" whose story I am sharing with you for us to determine if he represents Responsibility or irResponsibility.

Most parents have high hopes and dreams for their sons and daughters. Minutes after the births of my children, I looked down into their sweet, innocent faces and dreamed they would be successful as doctors, lawyers, scientists, or even President of the United States. I hoped they would help save the world and make it a better place. As I studied their blank canvases, deep down I knew they would be Responsible and hard-working citizens of their towns, states, and the world as they developed into a special work of art all their own.

EDDIE - Solomon and Henrietta had similar hopes and dreams for their third child, Eddie, as they gazed into his small face after his birth. They were from a blue collar world. Sol was a truck driver and Henrietta, a housewife, and they lived in a modest house down a dirt road. They were Responsible parents and expected Responsibility from each of their six children.

Responsibility was the last thing on Eddie's mind when he dropped out of school at 16 to work in a cannery. He never returned to finish high school, never attended a single college class, nor received any kind of degree. The only vision he had was tunnel; his blinders were on, and all he could see was surfing.

What could he possibly do that would be more irResponsible? He figured it out; he bought a surfboard as soon as possible with what little money he earned from the cannery. Most likely he rationalized his purchase because he and his younger brother Clyde had always constructed their surfboards out of marine plywood, and now he deserved to have his own real surfboard. Eddie's actions appear to reinforce my initial perception of him as an irResponsible surfer dude.

Eddie and his new surfboard were soon inseparable. With each horizon came a fresh adventure where they escaped to conquer the next and best wave no one else dared to even attempt.

The only other activities besides surfing Eddie focused on were playing his guitar, singing, and songwriting; however, Sol still tried to instill Responsibility when he informed Eddie their yard had to be mowed and all chores completed before he could go surfing, no matter how high the waves. Determined to appease his Dad, Eddie would mow at 1:00 – 2:00 a.m. as the car headlights beamed on the grass to earn him the privilege to surf the big waves. (Which I'm sure wasn't popular with their neighbors.)

Once Clyde cut school and rushed to the beach in time to witness big brother Eddie ride the biggest wave ever, so powerful it shook the ground beneath Clyde's feet. While others surfed with nervous expressions on their faces, Eddie cruised down the most ferocious wave with a beaming smile on his. He often surfed in dangerous areas where many regularly lost their lives. His lack of fear coupled with the refusal to never deny a wave, created the maxim, "Eddie Would Go."

Eddie took the biggest waves riding them better than anyone. ~~~Peter Cole, Eddie's Friend

My children occasionally participated in activities I perceived as irResponsible. They often left me with words like, "Don't worry. I can do it," ringing in my ears. Ironically, those were the last words Eddie spoke as he paddled out into the Pacific Ocean on his surfboard, never to be seen again, as he became one with the ocean and the waves he loved so much.

The most extensive air/water hunt in Hawaiian history took place to search for Eddie Aikau, but he was lost to the ocean. The ocean was his life and ended up to be his final resting place. It would seem even in death he was irResponsible, but you haven't heard the rest of Eddie's story.

Eddie Aikau's name is synonymous with the principles of taking care of one's fellow man and upholding Hawaiian culture and family values with dignity and boldness. He has become the benchmark for all big wave riders to measure themselves, and he is most definitely classified as a hero.

Eddie did have an overwhelming passion for surfing and loved the ocean much like his Hawaiian ancestors who developed the art of riding waves for pleasure. He was born on the Hawaiian Island of Maui, but his parents later moved to Honolulu on Oahu Island to give their children the opportunity for a better life.

Eddie spent a lot of time surfing and knew about the enormous number of people who lost their lives around Honolulu and the North Shore area where the world's most challenging surf was, and still is, located. He was deeply concerned and felt an overwhelming Responsibility to take appropriate actions to keep people safe from his beloved ocean.

He talked and pleaded with local city and county leaders around Honolulu and the North Shore until he finally persuaded them to appoint him to be a lifeguard. This took place in the 1960s when having lifeguards on the beach was a totally foreign concept. After his appointment, he covered all the beaches from Sunset Beach to Haleiwa driving back and forth in an old hearse saving locals and tourists as well as keeping suicidal servicemen stationed in Pearl Harbor in check.

He saved hundreds of lives, some say as many as 300, never losing even one person on his watch, as he often defied waves 30 feet tall and higher. He went where others would not dare go to save a life. This lead people to say, "Eddie Would Go," referring to his bravery and willingness to help his fellow man above-and-beyond what was expected. This now-famous aphorism is on t-shirts, cups, and hats as well as other items to pay honor to his principles.

During a surfing contest in the area in 1967, Eddie took on a 40-foot wave (comparable to a four-story building) and prevailed. During this ride, a photographer for *Life Magazine* snapped his picture and put him on the cover. In 1971 his peers voted him Lifeguard of the Year, and in 1977 he triumphantly surfed to victory as he won the Duke Kahanamoku Invitational Surfing Championship.

Eddie felt a keen Responsibility to help eradicate discrimination but was often pricked by its thorns. You see, Eddie did not at all resemble the typical surfer dude stereotype of his time. He did not have sun-bleached hair, blue eyes, or the cliché (totally dude) stoner voice.

He was quiet and shy, and being a native Hawaiian, had long shaggy dark hair, dark eyes, and dark skin. When he visited Durban, South Africa, for a pro-surfing contest, Eddie was not allowed to check into his hotel because of his dark skin. He even had to get a special permit to surf Durban's "whites only" beach. Understanding how ignorance often leads to discrimination, Eddie felt a Responsibility to mediate fights and misunderstandings between native Hawaiians and Australians, which he often did.

Eddie Aikau was extremely proud of his heritage and did his share to promote native Hawaiian culture. Many believe the Hawaiian Islands were first populated by Marquesas, who rowed to the Hawaiian Islands in canoes during the 3rd century. Later in the 1300s, Tahitians followed, conquering the inhabitants, after traveling over 2,500 miles across the Pacific Ocean. In 1976, to promote Hawaiian pride, a group took the journey in a canoe to Tahiti, accompanied by protective vessels.

Another journey was planned to take place on March 16, 1978; this time without protection. Eddie was selected to be one of the 17 crew members. They headed out on the evening of March 16 for a 30-day trek towards Tahiti aboard their 62 foot, 7-ton canoe straight into a gusty trade wind.

They didn't get very far as they rode over and through 15-foot swells. These swells hit hard and without mercy causing the canoe to spring a leak and capsize around midnight. The crew clung to the canoe the rest of the night. In the morning Eddie announced he would head out for help towards the nearest island, believed to be around 13 miles away. The last words Eddie had said before he and his surfboard paddled out of sight were, "Don't worry. I can do it." A few hours after Eddie left, a Hawaiian commercial pilot, flying over the area, spotted the crew and canoe from the air and radioed for help. The Coast Guard soon arrived to save the remaining 16 crew members, but 31-year-old Eddie Aikau was never seen again.

No matter what your talents or skills, you can be Responsible and proud of what you do and who you are. Eddie was a Responsible surfer dude and hero. In 1985, a Quiksilver Big Wave Invitational surfing competition called The Eddie was initiated on Oahu's North Shore in his memory. Each year since that time from December 1 to February 28, twenty-something invited surfers wait to see if there will be 30-40-foot waves to last long enough for a two-round competition. Jet skis are not allowed to tow surfers. Only eight times in the 29 years since the competition started have the waves cooperated. The first winner of the competition was Clyde, Eddie's little brother, who won the competition with Eddie's ten-year-old surfboard. Clyde is now in his 60s, still lives in Hawaii, and still surfs. The other seven winners beside Clyde Aikau were Denton Miyamura (Hawaii); Keone Downing (Hawaii); Ross Clarke-Jones (Australia); Kelly Slater (Florida); Noah Johnson (Hawaii); Bruce Irons (Hawaii); and Greg Long (California).

During the days of February 11 - February 24, 2014, I was fortunate to walk along many of Eddie Aikau's Hawaiian beaches and gaze out into the same ocean he surfed and loved. I believe I felt his spirit of Responsibility. I thanked God for his life and the sacrifices he had made, especially giving his life, for others. As the ocean breeze caressed my face and the warm sand covered my toes, my own spirit was renewed. I also found my hopes and dreams I had for me and my children were restored by the life-force of this Responsible surfer dude.

As you pave your High Road with those proper materials, you will encounter a lot of people. You'll meet some good people, which if you stumble and fall, will have their roads paved with Respect, Rules, Resourcefulness, and Responsibility. They will stop to help you if you're stranded on the side of the road.

* * *

COMMENTS AND NOTES ON
HOW TO PAVE YOUR HIGH ROAD WITH RESPECT,
RULES, RESOURCEFULNESS, AND RESPONSIBILITY.

CHAPTER SEVEN - IF YOU'RE LEADING THE CARAVAN, MAKE SURE YOUR GPS IS WORKING (BE A GOOD LEADER)

WARREN - As a leader can you choose integrity without having to sacrifice power and money? Leaders with integrity know how to create a culture of trust. Warren Buffett, in an address to a group of Harvard Business School MBAs, said when he hires he looks for integrity, intelligence, and a high energy level.

I was saddened to find out a poll by Watson Wyatt showed fewer than two out of every five employees said they trusted their senior managers. If you're in corporate management or in a leadership role, you shouldn't have to apologize for your title. Since a reputation can be lost in a moment and take years to rebuild, it's important to always protect integrity.

JACK - Jack Forney of Forney Industries from Fort Collins, Colorado, started his business in Des Moines, Iowa, right after he married his high school sweetheart, Patricia. Years later he was faced with a choice of whether or not to go along with a deceptive practice to misrepresent the power of his company's battery chargers like his competition was. Jack Took The High Road and told the truth.

At first sales went down but the truth helped the company in the long run as he continued to build his integrity. Jack was also known to encourage those with a disability to work for his company as he "found them to be more loyal, have less absenteeism, and many times do a better job." Jack said true success is built on the work of others; he felt God gave him direction in his life, and that was his success. I believe he kept his GPS set in the proper High Road direction. As I was updating his story in mid-December, 2014, I was saddened to find he had passed away a few weeks earlier on December 3.

What do High Road Leaders have their GPS set on? Are you a good leader? What makes a good leader? That's a question asked since the beginning of time. A lot of research has been conducted, and there's still no perfect recipe. We can agree on traits we believe leaders should possess like honesty, strong work ethic, intelligence, good communication skills, and the ability to inspire. Yet having all these traits cannot guarantee you'll be a great leader.

Leaders, in general, tend to be a little more intelligent, a little better looking, a little taller, and a little more emotionally stable than non-leaders, but there have been great leaders who aren't so smart, aren't too good to look at, short, and may have been mentally ill.

We know there are things we do not like to see in our leaders. If we do not like leaders who are emotionally unstable, then we should seek appropriate counseling if we become unstable.

Two qualities I personally don't like to see in a leader are complaining and micromanaging. Therefore, when I am in a leadership role, I work hard to battle those two issues. I try to remember the time I was told when we complain, 80% of those we complain to don't empathize with us and could care less what we are going through. I was also told almost all of the remaining 20% are actually glad we're going through all the bad things we're going through.

~~~

What work I have done I have done because it has been play. If it had been work, I shouldn't have done it.

Who was it who said, "Blessed is the man who has found his work"? Whoever it was he had the right idea in his mind. Mark you, he says his work--not somebody else's work. The work that is really a man's own work is play and not work at all. Cursed is the man who has found some other man's work and cannot lose it. When we talk about the great workers of the world, we really mean the great players of the world. The fellows who groan and sweat under the weary load of toil that they bear never can hope to do anything great. How can they when their souls are in a ferment of revolt against the employment of their hands and brains? The product of slavery, intellectual or physical, can never be great. ~~~Mark Twain, "A Humorist Confession," *New York Times*, 11.26.1905

~~~

TANYA - *Forbes Magazine,* back in December of 2012, featured an article written by Tanya Prive on leadership that listed 10 qualities that make a great leader. Those qualities are honesty, ability to delegate, communication, sense of humor, confidence, commitment, positive attitude, creativity, intuition, and ability to inspire. I would advise looking up this article and reading it to help you set your High Road GPS.

ALAN - I recently found an old notebook packed away in a box along with some other books and materials from my teaching days at Shelton State Community College in Tuscaloosa, Alabama. In the notebook were some notes I had made about a book I'd read by Alan Loy McGinnis titled, *Bringing out the Best in People* along with the quote, "Helping other people grow can become life's greatest joy." I like that quote. I had read his book when I was selected to be part of a certified training team to teach TQM (Total Quality Management) classes in the early 1990s to the staff, faculty, and administration of the college. I had also written down 12 Rules he had said to follow when bringing out the best in people. Looking back over the list, two, in particular, resonated with me, although all 12 were excellent. The two favorites of mine were "to create an atmosphere where failure is not fatal," and "take steps to keep your own motivation high." As leaders, we must also remember it's important to nurture our own motivation. This is another reason I felt compelled to write this book.

As you motivate yourself, you may be instilling leadership qualities in others without realizing you're doing so. You simply enter and finish the race you've been given, as shown in the life of Jeffrey Zaslow.

What would you attempt to do if you knew there was no way you would fail? You never know when you will have your last opportunity to enter a race that gives you the opportunity to go on a journey that provides great enjoyment for you and those around you.

JEFFREY - When I read online Jeffrey Zaslow was killed in an automobile accident driving back from an event which had promoted his most recent book, it really affected me. Jeffrey Zaslow was the man who encouraged Randy Pausch to write the book, *The Last Lecture*. He also helped co-write this inspirational book. When Zaslow was a writer for the *Wall Street Journal*, he wrote many articles which inspired his readers to be better people. He wrote about people seeking meaning for their lives. His race was not a popular one as he was often criticized for writing fluff stories instead of the hard-hitting, survival of the fittest ones the other Wall Street Journal writers penned. In the last years of his life, he sought individuals to help them write about how they overcame diversities (Randy Pausch, Congresswoman Gabby Giffords, and airline pilot Capt. Chesley "Sully" Sullenberger).

While reading the book, *The Art of Racing in the Rain* (not written by Zaslow), I wrote down the inspirational comment, "There's no shame in losing a race; the shame is in never entering the race because of being afraid of failure." Jeffrey Zaslow was never afraid to enter his race to write and encourage others to write to inspire. He and his work will be missed. Let his life inspire us all to not wait until it's too late to enter our races, especially if we're afraid of failure. A leader is not afraid of failure.

 **HIGH ROAD HINT #8 – A GOOD LEADER IS NOT AFRAID OF FAILURE.**

HUBERT - Speaking of races and failures, Senator and Vice-President Hubert H. Humphrey is someone who was never afraid of failure even though some may think of him as a failure, as he ran the race for President of the United States but never won.

Let's look at another race Vice President Humphrey won. He was the driving force behind the Civil Rights Act of 1964. President

Johnson got the main credit for the passage of the Civil Rights Act, but Democrat Hubert H. Humphrey was the one who tried and tried and finally succeeded in getting the votes to pass the Act and stop the 54-day filibuster after he garnished the help of Republican Senator Everett Dirksen.

When the bill was signed in 1964, over 50 years ago, the first two pens handed out at the ceremony at the White House went to Humphrey of Minnesota and Dirksen of Illinois, the two senators who made it happen. Don't be afraid of failure. Set your GPS for the High Road and enter your race you were meant to run.

***

COMMENTS AND NOTES ON HOW TO KEEP YOUR GPS WORKING AND TO BE A GOOD LEADER.

_____

_____

_____

CHAPTER EIGHT - BEWARE OF SKUNKS, DEER, AND SUNDAY DRIVERS (AKA GOSSIPS, BULLIES, AND GOOF-OFFS)

As you drive along The High Road, you will see a variety of wildlife like turkeys, pheasant, quail, possums, skunks, raccoons, and deer. Sometimes they are on the edge of the road, and sometimes they are far away. You soon learn even those far away can within seconds get in front of you and be in your way. It's important to look out for them and not let them slow you down or ruin your drive.

SKUNKS

Driving along Our Professional High Road, we may notice an odor in the air caused by skunks. So what can we say about skunks? Well, we can start by making the following statements.

1. SKUNKS ARE CUTE.

They have every right to strut the earth with their cute little black and white body and fluffy tail.

2. THEY DO A LOT OF GOOD THINGS.

Skunks eat things dangerous to us like black widow and brown recluse spiders and rats. They even eat leaves which could mean less raking if you allowed skunks to congregate around your house.

3. YOU CAN SMELL THEM A MILE AWAY.

Their smell is one of nature's worst smells. This smell can make you sick or even cause temporary blindness. Their smell is not so easy to get rid of.

4. THEY HAVE A SELF-DEFENSE MECHANISM.

Their main natural predator is the great horned owl which can't smell very well.

5. YOU CAN'T BE AROUND THEM WITHOUT THE SMELL RUBBING OFF ON YOU.

They can shoot their smell up to 15 feet away. If you get too close to them, the smell can make you cry.

6. THEY HAVE A SEEMINGLY ENDLESS SUPPLY OF STINKY STUFF TO SHARE WITH YOU.

That stinky smell will even return when whatever it's attached to gets wet.

7. ON THE PROFESSIONAL HIGH ROAD, A SKUNK IS A GOSSIP.

We should treat gossips in the workplace similar to how we treat skunks. Stay clear of them. When they try to dump something on you, run! Don't get mad, but when some of their smell gets on you, know the formula to get rid of the smell.

If you propose to speak, always ask yourself: is it true, is it necessary, is it kind. ~~~Buddha

Do not listen to stinky gossip. Instead, change the subject. Do not share what did get on you, which means you must cleanse your mind to focus on something more important.

DEER

On Your Professional High Road, you will encounter managers or co-workers who step on you or run over you to make them look good. They (like deer) come out of nowhere. They are workplace bullies. They don't travel alone and can ruin your day. Always remember they are deadly because they have no respect for you. They focus on themselves and their agendas. If you get in their way, they knock you out of the way in the hopes you will fall back down on The Low Road.

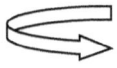

HIGH ROAD HINT #9 – BEWARE OF WORKPLACE BULLIES. THEY ARE DEADLY AND HAVE NO RESPECT FOR YOU.

There will be many opportunities for bullies to run over you or run you off the road. These opportunities will present themselves to you in all areas of your life. It could be your boss, co-worker, spouse, child, parent, friend, next door neighbor, business partner, banker, financial advisor, psychiatrist, and the list goes on and on. All of them could be looking to bully you for their advantage and vice versa; you may find the opportunity presents itself for you to bully them to get ahead. It's frustrating to be bullied and heartbreaking to find out it's happening to someone you care about. You may even bully those around you and not even recognize what you're doing. After all, your perception may be stronger than reality.

TOMMY - As a first grader in Zion, Illinois, I got to know a lot of child bullies. For several weeks I observed a bully named Tommy, who terrorized child after child on the way to school in the mornings. He pushed them around, knocked them into snow banks, and teased them until they cried. I had made up my mind I was going to avoid him, but I wasn't going to let him bully me. Whenever he came my way, I walked to the other side of the road to another sidewalk.

One morning as I turned the corner to enter the school building, Tommy came up and shoved me from behind. I didn't say anything or do anything and kept walking. He ran up to stand in front of me to block my path. I still didn't say a word and avoided his gaze. He then told me I couldn't come around him and he was going to knock me down into the snow. Still without saying a word, I put down my books and with the element of surprise I ran full force toward Tommy and tackled him. We landed in a snowbank with me sitting on his stomach. I sat on him for a few seconds, got up, dusted the snow off my clothes, retrieved my books, and walked into the school building still without saying a word. I never had any more trouble with Tommy.

I don't know if I Took The High Road in dealing with this childhood bully. I do know it was important to me to take up for myself and not let him intimidate me or ruin my 1st-grade year. I also know for the rest of the school year I never saw him bully another child.

Martin Luther King, Jr. had a dream, and so do I. My dream is that workplace bullying will disappear.
~~~Judy Barker Austin

Now let me tell you about a guy named Carl.

CARL - Carl was definitely on The High Road. He had it all-- good looks, intelligence, education, important political contacts, a satisfying career, close family, and esteem of those he worked closely with as well as people nationwide.

With his thick hair, good looks, and 6'4" stature, Carl commanded attention wherever he went. An avid reader, he had read at least two books a week since the age of eight and graduated from high school when he was only 16.

When he went away to attend college, he spent time his first day on campus with the university's president. After being voted SGA President for two years in a row, he continued to have contact with not only his university's president but another president as well.

His connections with a Justice of the U. S. Supreme Court afforded the young college student a private talk with the President of the United States in the Oval Office. Carl's college roommates ended up being influential adults--Virgil Lee Bedsole, Head of Archives History at Louisiana State University, and James Coley Etheridge, an attorney in Washington. Carl received a bachelor's degree and a law degree.

After college, he owned his own lucrative law firm before he ran for Congress. He was successful and was an esteemed member of Congress for 16 years. Carl was side by side with John F. Kennedy, Richard Nixon, and Gerald Ford and recognized for his public service by being the first recipient of the Kennedy Profiles in Courage Award. An award-winning television documentary was written and produced about his life, and Jacqueline Kennedy Onassis encouraged him to write his memoirs in an autobiography, which he did.

It's easy for us to look at successful people like Carl and wonder why it's so much easier for people with his position and power to get on and stay on The High Road, than it is for us.

It would appear Carl was born with a silver spoon in his mouth. He most likely came from a wealthy family, with plenty of influence, who gave him everything. He probably didn't care about others and only looked out for his own selfish interests as he climbed up to get on The High Road to success. After all, don't the Carls in the world get where they are as a result of bullying and running over others? Haven't we witnessed these types of successes in the workplace?

Now back to Carl . . . Carl Atwood Elliott was NOT born with a silver spoon in his mouth, and he stepped on and progressed on The High Road WITHOUT running over others or bullying others to get where he needed to go to be successful. He was born on a farm to a poor family right outside Vina, Alabama, (my hometown) where he was the oldest of nine children.

When he went away to college, he had all his belongings in a cardboard box and only a couple of dollars and some change in his pocket. He and his friend, Spud, planned to walk over 100 miles to Tuscaloosa, Alabama, to attend the University of Alabama.

Before they could get started, they ran into local store owner, J. W. Rodgers, who gave money to preacher H. T. Vaughn to drive the boys to Tuscaloosa. They arrived in Tuscaloosa in Brother Vaughn's two-seater Ford one year into the Great Depression with no plans, no application, and no money to pay for their college education. More importantly, though, was they had the dream to graduate from college.

Carl saw University of Alabama's President, George H. Denny, on his first day in Tuscaloosa, but I'm sure it wasn't under the circumstances you previously might have thought. President Denny was a tough financial and political leader who kept the University open during the Great Depression when many other college presidents all around the country closed their college doors. He was known to rule the University of Alabama with an iron fist and steel will. Carl found his way to President Denny's office, but it wasn't a pleasant social meeting. It was a humiliating meeting for Carl, as he was told by President Denny to go back home and come back in a year or two when he'd saved up enough money to afford a college education.

Carl and Spud spent their first night in Tuscaloosa sleeping outside, under a truck, in the drizzling rain. The truck belonged to Harry Hughes, Superintendent of Maintenance and Grounds at the University. They had stopped by there looking for work the superintendent didn't have. Harry told his wife, "Here are two fellows who have enough gall to think they're gonna enter the University of Alabama without a dime."

Carl did attend college but never lived in a luxurious fraternity house; in fact, he was virtually homeless. He convinced a lady to let him stay in a place rent free until she rented it. When she rented it, Carl and Spud had to leave. Since rent was not something they could afford, they hunted up another free place to live. Behind an old campus observatory, they found an abandoned building covered in vines. That's where they met up with Virgil Lee Bedsole and James Coley Etheridge. They were in a similar situation of having the dream to attend college without enough money for a place to live. They all promised to keep their living conditions a secret. They didn't want to be thrown out of the abandoned building they lived in even though it had no air, heat, running water, or electricity.

Many of Carl's fellow classmates disparaged him as a hillbilly and moved away from him when he sat near them in class. Hillbilly Carl worked five jobs his first college semester to pay his tuition, took 18 hours while maintaining an A average, and was able to send a little money home to help his parents out with his brothers and sisters.

Carl was the first University of Alabama SGA President elected without the machine, which was made up of sororities and fraternities who banded together and decided most of what happened on campus, and especially who would become SGA President. This machine is still very much in force dominating campus policies at the University of Alabama today. He represented the have-nots and those shunned by the sororities and fraternities. He threw a dance for the non-sorority girls and almost 850 showed up. This was the first time many of them had ever been to a dance. The have-not hillbilly candidate won the election by a margin of 2 to 1.

As SGA President, Carl did spend a lot of time with University of Alabama President Denny, but not for social reasons. Carl fought for change; Denny didn't want change. For example, Carl resented students being forced to buy their books from the high-priced, privately-owned supply store. Carl Elliott thought the store should be owned by the students and prices should be lowered. He felt owners of the supply store took advantage of students. Carl investigated the circumstances and found President Denny had a financial interest in the supply store; so the ownership stayed the same.

Carl was victorious in one regard as he convinced the owners of the store to lower prices. He fought to have benches installed on campus for the less influential students to sit on when they courted. Fraternities and sororities had nice courting rooms; the less fortunate courted outside, sitting on blankets, along the hillside.

Because of a note written by Supreme Court Justice Hugo Black, a native of Alabama and who had graduated from the University's School of Law, Carl was allowed to see President Franklin Delano Roosevelt in his Oval Office. Carl went to talk to President Roosevelt about the tragedy of smart young people not able to attend college because of lack of money. Carl then testified before Congress to try to convince them to provide federal scholarships for college students. It would be over 20 years later before Congressman Carl Elliott would sponsor and get through the House of Representatives and Senate the first federal bill to provide help for financially-disadvantaged students. It wouldn't be scholarships, but it was federally-backed low-interest loans.

Carl graduated from the University of Alabama in 1933 with his bachelor's degree and a law degree in 1936. He later said the hardest thing he had ever done in his life was to get those two degrees. It wasn't because of his intelligence but rather because of his lack of financial resources. It took every ounce of his strength and energy during those six years to get his education. Carl had grit and determination and did not let anything stand in the way of his dreams.

Carl Elliott Took The High Road not for himself but also for the poor and disadvantaged. He was determined for everyone with enough mental intelligence to have the chance for a college education no matter their social or financial background. He left the University of Alabama determined to continue to fight for the poorest and most disadvantaged. To accomplish this, he felt he needed to go to Washington, D.C. as a member of Congress; so that's what he did.

As a result of getting on The High Road and staying on The High Road, he co-authored the NDEA (National Defense Education Act) and fought hard to get it passed making it possible for students to go to college through student loans. If you went to college after 1958 on a federal student loan or were helped by a federal grant, you have Carl to thank. I know I do. He was an inspiration to me as I grew up and is one of the greatest examples I can come up with of someone who lived his entire life on The High Road.

Carl Elliott continued to speak up for the disadvantaged and the poor. It didn't matter to him where they came from or the color of their skin. Because this was not a popular belief for a southern politician to have in the 1960s, he was bullied. His fifth attempt for a seat in Congress and his run for governor of Alabama were both ruined by bullies. These campaigns left him over $500,000 in debt and his congressional pension spent. He went back to continue his law practice in Jasper, Alabama, stubbornly refusing to file bankruptcy. He lost his home and had to rent it back from the bank. He applied for teaching positions at universities around the state, but political bullies blocked that opportunity as well, as they suggested to university officials if they hired Carl, their funding would be drastically cut.

Carl continued to keep on The High Road as he didn't harbor bitterness against the bullies who caused him a total public defeat, intense public scorn, personal abuse, and financial ruin. He never saw himself as a victim.

Years later Boston Globe reporter, Wil Haygood, (who is also known for writing the New York Times bestseller, *The Butler*), came to Jasper, Alabama, looking for Congressman Carl Elliott. He wanted to interview the ex-Congressman for an article he was writing on Adam Clayton Powell, Jr., former chairman of the powerful Education and Labor Committee of the 1960s. Haygood may have expected to find the ex-Congressman living comfortably in a three-story mansion with white columns, drinking a mint julep, and waited on hand-and-foot by a bevy of servants. Instead, he was told by a few people in town former Congressman Carl Elliott was dead.

Well, Carl Elliott was not dead; nor did he live in a mansion. The reporter found him alone in a small frame house living on social security. After spending two days with Carl Elliott, Haygood decided to also do an article on him to share how he had helped financially-disadvantaged students receive college educations. A photographer flew down to Alabama to take the former Congressman's picture, and an article soon appeared in the Boston Globe and Chicago Tribune Newspapers.

Not long after the article was published, Carl Elliott started receiving letters from professionals all over the United States thanking him for his work in setting up the college loan program for those with financial need. They shared how they couldn't have gotten where they were without those student loans. They were glad to know the person responsible for starting the program. Many sent money to Carl to help him because he now was in financial need. They sympathized with him but also admired his stand for civil rights and how he helped the disadvantaged, which had cost him everything.

When Carl Elliott's former legislative assistant, Mary Jolley, found out Caroline Kennedy wanted to honor a person in public service who had sacrificed for the common good and had paid the price for exhibiting the courage of their convictions, she knew her former boss should be the first honoree for the award. Ms. Jolley got together with an attorney and filled out the paperwork to do what it took to nominate her former boss and friend. There were 5,000 nominations for the honor.

Carl Atwood Elliott won. He was the very first recipient of the JFK Profiles in Courage Award. He flew to Boston to accept the award with about 50 family members and friends.

Senator Ted Kennedy, who presented the award, said this concerning Carl Elliott.

> *"Carl Elliott has demonstrated the true meaning of political courage throughout his career. He met the challenges of the 50s and 60s head on, working tirelessly against injustice and promoting opportunity for all Americans. He led the successful effort to enact the historic National Defense Education Act of 1958, which helped to make college education accessible to all Americans without regard to their race or economic status. He persevered despite the fact that his stands were anathema in the reactionary political climate of Alabama at the time. Ultimately they cost him his career. Like many of the leaders described in Profiles in Courage, Carl Elliott has suffered heavily for his ideals. We hope the Profile in Courage Award will bring him at least some small measure of the recognition and respect he deserves for serving his country so well in one of the most difficult eras of our history."*

In his acceptance speech Carl said, *"Early in my life I became aware that brains and ability knew no economic, racial, or other distinction. When the Good Lord distributed intellectual ability, I am sure he did so without regard to the color or station in life of the recipient."*

He concluded his acceptance by stating, *"There were those who said that I was ahead of my time, but they were wrong. I believe that I was always behind the times that ought to be."*

Carl Elliott was loved and respected by his remaining family members, as well as by those he had worked with. His nephew, Steve Elliott, is an editor and accomplished writer who resides in Seattle, Washington. I emailed him back in 2008 to see if he'd share some thoughts concerning his uncle. I received the following response immediately.

"There are two types of politicians: one who appeals to our higher natures, and one who appeals to our dark sides. Uncle Carl was definitely the first type. I was only six years old when my uncle, then an eight-term Congressman (from the old 7th District in Alabama), ran for Governor of the state against Lurleen Wallace, who was running as proxy for her racist demagogue husband, George. Even now, almost 42 years later, I can remember how Uncle Carl's campaign against the forces of fear and racism opened my young eyes to a side of human nature that isn't so pretty. The defaced campaign billboards . . . the literature ripped up and thrown back at campaign workers . . . the bomb threats at his speeches. It was an intense initiation for a six-year-old, and I never forgot how it feels to confront ignorance and prejudice. Uncle Carl was eventually vindicated -- 25 years later -- when he won the very first John F. Kennedy Profiles in Courage Award. Nobody ever deserved it more. Uncle Carl refused to take the 'low road' of pandering to racism and bigotry, even though it would have been the easy thing to do, especially in 1966. He had principles he believed in, and he wouldn't compromise those principles or waver from them. His refusal to take the low road, and his insistence on doing what was right, cost him not just his political career, but his personal fortune and Congressional retirement -- he poured everything he had into the fight, which he unfortunately lost at that time. (The changes which Uncle Carl already knew were inevitable did indeed go ahead and happen, just a couple years later than they would have if he'd been elected.) I talked a lot with Uncle Carl in his later years, and when he got on the subject of standing up for what he believed in, even at great personal cost, he'd quote to me an old chestnut from Henry Clay: "I'd rather be right than be president."

Carl Elliott's last nine years of his life were "very satisfying and productive, and a lot of good things came his way," according to his ex-legislative assistant.

Ms. Jolley also said, *"Carl Elliott believed the way things are is not the way they have to be. He believed change could be made. Although fate had dealt him a hard hand of political failure, and he'd had physical suffering and pain--Carl Elliott was not a victim. He never became a victim. He was always victorious. He went to his grave believing that in the sweep of history that he would be treated fairly and that the things he stood for would be seen as significant and long lasting."*

Alabama Public TV did an award-winning documentary on him called, *Conscience of a Congressman,* and he wrote his autobiography titled, *The Cost of Courage: The Journey of an American Congressman,* after being encouraged to by Jacqueline Kennedy Onassis.

What a wonderful story about a man who got on The High Road and stayed on The High Road without stepping on others, and although Carl Elliott was run over and bullied, he ended up victorious without retaliating against his bullies.

Many good and decent people are turning their heads and doing nothing when they observe workplace bullying. In the 1930s and 1940s, many good and decent people also turned their heads and did nothing about the evil deeds surrounding the tragedies of the Holocaust. The same thing happened as numerous young females quit their jobs in the 1980s and 1990s to fall into further economic hopelessness rather than submit to sexual advances. They felt powerless to do anything while those who could have made a difference simply turned their heads and pretended it wasn't happening.

Sexual harassment wasn't so much about sex as it was about power. Those committing the harassment often got more and more powerful, and no one stepped in to make a stand. That's exactly what is happening today with workplace bullying.

According to a 2000 study by Wayne State University in Michigan, one in six American workers experience some sort of bullying on the job. A 2014 survey by the Workplace Bullying Institute (WBI) reported 72% of employers deny, discount, encourage, rationalize, or defend workplace bullying.

Working in supervision for state government August 2005 – October 2007, I saw bullying on a daily basis. When I refused to participate in the bullying and stood up to protect those who were being bullied, it ultimately cost my job.

For sexual harassment to become illegal and stop spreading, people had to stand up to the people committing the harassment and punish them. Today almost every organization whether in the private, public, government, or nonprofit sector, has sexual harassment training. Policies are in place and enforced. No longer are people turning their heads. At some point, people stopped turning their heads to the travesties of the Holocaust to stop it. When are we going to stop turning our heads concerning workplace bullying and put a stop to it and stop rewarding and promoting bullying behaviors? Is there anything you're turning your head to that you believe is evil?

EDWARDS - W. Edwards Deming, whom I consider the Father of Total Quality Management, came up with 14 Points in his Philosophy of Quality Management. Number eight on that list was to "eliminate fear." When workers fear they can't be themselves, they can't reach their potential. Bullies do not want others to reach their potential because that would diminish their own worth or how others perceive their worth. Workers who are afraid do not ask questions, which can result in preventable mistakes and disasters. Bullies would rather have the disasters happen so they can correct a behavior or situation rather than prevent the mistakes by encouraging an atmosphere of trust and acceptance. They get a high from corrective rather than preventive procedures.

What's really ironic is bullies often create the situations they want credit for repairing. They throw mud at you and then say, "Oh you poor thing, let me help you. Give me those dirty clothes. I'll wash and iron them and get them right back to you." As you stand there exposed with everyone staring at you with pity, the bully tells everyone how she came to your rescue and how she's going to handle the situation and save the day. When you get your clothes back from the bully and put them on, you're grateful for the clothes even though they have a few stains that didn't quite come out. You know you're expected to thank the bully, but you're reluctant to do so or join in with the accolades because you remember how the mud got on you in the first place. You also remember how when you first got to work that morning, your clothes were stain free.

If you've been a recipient of the mud from a bully who never gets reprimanded or rebuked for her behavior, you start to feel the only way to get on The High Road is to mimic the bad behavior. But do you have to?

I say NO. You don't have to bully others or allow yourself to be a victim to get on and remain on The High Road. You should have respect for yourself and for others.

You're somebody if you don't think so yourself.
~~~An African-American Proverb

SUSAN - According to Dr. Susan Futterman, in her book, *When You Work for a Bully*, the definition of bullying is . . . "using one's authority to undermine, frighten, or intimidate another person, often leaving the victim feeling afraid, powerless, incompetent, and ashamed."

How do you know if you, or someone you know, is being bullied? Shown below are some tactics used by bullies. The more behaviors are present, the more of a chance you are either working for or working with a bully.

1. Use physical or verbal abuse
2. Invade personal space
3. Humiliate others in front of co-workers
4. Threaten without firing
5. Demote for no reason
6. Exclude others from necessary meetings
7. Withhold important job-needed information
8. Bombard with unwarranted criticism
9. Arbitrarily change deadlines
10. Undercut authority
11. Not answer calls or emails
12. Refuse to recognize positive contributions, achievements, or intrinsic value
13. If forced to say something positive, will follow with a derogatory comment
14. Treats others as if they are invisible

Instead of advising you to immediately run at the bully, knock her down, and sit on her, I would advise you to consider doing these 7 things.

1. PUT YOUR HEALTH FIRST.

If the bullying is affecting your mental or physical health, get help. It's especially important to not believe the lies the bully is telling about you, and don't let those lies add stress to your life.

2. DOCUMENT.

Write down everything. Be sure to include dates, witnesses, and specifics. Include any health-related conditions and appointments. This information will come in handy if you decide to talk to the bully, higher authorities, or an attorney.

3. ANALYZE.

Analyze your behavior. Is the person a bully because they're criticizing you for no reason or is your job performance not up to par?

4. TALK TO THE BULLY.

Do this only if you can do it in a calm and confident manner. Maybe she doesn't realize she's bullying you. Use the facts from your documentation, if necessary.

5. TALK TO A HUMAN RESOURCE MANAGEMENT REPRESENTATIVE OR HIGHER AUTHORITY.

If your attempt(s) to talk to the bully failed, go up the chain of command. Again, use facts from your documentation.

6. CONTINUE TO DOCUMENT.

Document what happened in your talks with the bully and HRM or the bully's boss.

7. PICK YOUR BATTLES.

Decide what you're willing to fight for. You deserve to be treated with respect. If no one on the job helps you, you have to decide whether to go to a lawyer or look for another job. Talking to a counselor or psychologist is also helpful.

Bullying shows a lack of Respect. If you're paving Your High Road with proper materials, as discussed previously in Chapter Six, you should definitely have Respect as one of your materials. Show Respect for all people, no matter what their age or station in life. I've always believed we should work hard trying to better ourselves, but that still doesn't make us any better than anyone else.

A good resource for information on workplace bullying is workplacebullying.org.

SUNDAY DRIVERS

You should also look out for those Sunday Drivers. They are the co-workers or bosses who drive slowly in the workplace. They constantly look for opportunities for leisure or sightseeing. It's also interesting they usually are totally oblivious when they bother you as they, just like the bullies, are only interested in their own agendas. In the workplace, they correspond to the goof-offs who can keep you from getting where you need to go at the time you need to be there.

Goof-offs even have their own day named after them. That day is March 22, which is called National Goof Off Day. Sunday Drivers (goof-offs) don't take their jobs as serious as you take your job.

Even when they say they do 100% of their job, we know what they're really saying is they only work 13% on Monday, 22% on Tuesday, 26% on Wednesday, 35% on Thursday, and 4% on Friday, which adds up to 100%. They, like the gossips (skunks) and deer (bullies), should be avoided.

* * *

COMMENTS AND NOTES ON
HOW TO AVOID SKUNKS, DEER AND SUNDAY
DRIVERS (AKA GOSSIPS, BULLIES, AND GOOF-OFFS).

_____

_____

_____

Part Three –
Take The High Road
In Your Personal Life

<u>Chapter Nine</u> - Since You're Traveling with Yourself, You'd Better Enjoy the Company (Like Yourself), Page 101.

<u>Chapter Ten</u> - Follow E.T.'s Advice and Phone Home (Develop and Nurture Personal Relationships, Page 107.

<u>Chapter Eleven</u> - Appreciate and Enjoy the Scenery (Be Thankful, and Live Your Life), Page 115.

<u>Chapter Twelve</u> - Avoid Road Rage (Forgive), Page 121.

BATTLE

I wake up lonely in a dark place--a deep, airless void
I hear footsteps and feel hot, damp breath
Traveling up my neck.

My legs are heavy, my arms are weak, and I cannot breathe
I desire to run toward light and air, but I fail
And I don't like myself.

My terrified mind thrashes as it screams for me to resist
I open my mouth to cry out for help, but I fail
And I don't like myself.

My soul is encircled with evil, and my free will melts
I gasp and struggle to repel advances, but I fail
And I don't like myself.

My hopes and dreams are plucked from my mind
I gallantly attack to win them back, but I fail.
And I don't like myself.

My now enervated mind whispers longingly for freedom
I want to be brave--to continue the fight, but I fail
And I don't like myself.

Apathy, gloom, and self-doubt smother me
I desire to pray for the return of my confidence, but I fail
And I don't like myself.

I am wretched, no longer yearning to make any
Difference for good, which makes me a coward
And I don't like myself.

I am conquered, am now a failure doomed to live
My worthless, pitiful life with nothing of use to offer
And I hate myself.

~ ~ ~Judy Barker Austin

CHAPTER NINE - SINCE YOU'RE TRAVELING WITH YOURSELF, YOU'D BETTER ENJOY THE COMPANY (LIKE YOURSELF)

CHERYL - Cheryl Nyland had trouble liking herself. She was born in Pennsylvania but moved to Minnesota when only five. Her father was abusive, so one year later her parents were divorced. Cheryl was constantly tormented that her father was never really in her life again. This caused her a lot of self-doubts even though she knew her mother loved her. When her mother remarried, they lived in a house they built themselves. There was no running water or electricity (imagine her winters in Minnesota). There was no indoor plumbing until after she went away to college. She had trouble liking her body image and as a freshman in high school weighed only 90 pounds even though as an adult she is 5' 7".

No matter how much you love someone, you must love yourself first and know your worth.
~~~Unknown Author

For a while it appeared she was overcoming her negative feelings towards herself and was starting to like herself more as she participated in track and field activities, became a cheerleader, and was the homecoming queen. She married a faithful, loving man and was close to finishing her college degree. Yes, it would seem things were better for Cheryl, but then "it" happened. A tragedy happened in her life that brought back all the depression, self-doubt, and insecurities. Her mother died. This event started her on a downward spiral of dislike for herself of which she couldn't escape.

Cheryl didn't receive her college degree even though she only needed to write one paper for one class to finish. She refused to use her education or her talents. Instead, she spent her time as a waitress and once had sex with five different cooks in one month. She continued to mask her dislike for herself and fill the holes within her to feel valid, worthy, and loved through continued promiscuity. She had sex with anyone, and everyone--young, old, educated, uneducated, employed, unemployed, men, women . . . She tried heroin and allowed a heroin addict to get her pregnant. Then she got an abortion, divorced her husband, and continued on her path of promiscuity.

She was definitely on The Low Road. None of these things did anything to numb the grief she felt because of her mother's death. She had nightmares she was killing her mother. Since she did not know the love of her father, she now felt her mother was the only one who had ever loved her. Since her mother was gone, her grief and depression told her she would never be loved like that again. She couldn't even share grief with her stepfather as he married soon after her mother's death and removed any evidence from his home that his previous wife had ever existed.

It was so important for Cheryl to like herself. Not only like herself but actually love herself. It's important for you to like yourself, as well. After all, think about it. Who will you be around on Your High Road of Life for the longest amount of time? Your parents, your siblings, your spouse? No--it's you.

There are a lot of things that can happen or things you can do that can make you feel like you don't like yourself. Like Cheryl, it could be the loss of a loved one. Or it could be a loss of employment, your physical appearance, financial pressures, drug and alcohol abuse, abuse to you or by you, end of a long-term relationship--to name a few.

~~~

God grant me the serenity to accept the things I cannot change; courage to change the things I can; and wisdom to know the difference.

Living one day at a time; enjoying one moment at a time; accepting hardships as the pathway to peace; taking, as He did, this sinful world as it is, not as I would have it; trusting that He will make all things right if I surrender to His will; that I may be reasonably happy in this life and supremely happy with Him forever in the next. Amen
~~~Reinhold Niebuhr

~~~

We are able to change some of these things, but some we must accept as the Serenity Prayer suggests. Epictetus said, "Make the best use of what is in your power, and take the rest as it happens," but Reinhold Niebuhr is credited with the Serenity Prayer and its impact on helping individuals accept themselves and in turn being able to help themselves. Many believe Niebuhr to be the most influential American theologian of the 20th century.

An interesting thing about accepting yourself is you can't run or drive away from yourself. People who don't like themselves and can't accept themselves often try to cover up their depression and anger through alcohol and drug abuse, sex, eating too little or too much, or reckless spending. Yet when the actions are finished nothing has changed, and they still find themselves in worse shape still riding along The Low Road.

Cheryl felt so lost she changed her last name to "Strayed." After hitting rock bottom several years after her mother's death, she was in a store and picked up a book about the Pacific Crest Trail. Something within her told her to hike the 1,100 miles from the Mojave Desert in California to the Oregon/Washington border on the Pacific Crest Trail. She was compelled to do this to help her find herself and somehow put to rest this grief over the death of her mother which was continuing to consume her.

Lost is what I was, and am, the difference so slight,
What once was only ignorance has morphed its way to fright.
I find myself discovering that work is way too hard:
A curse, a joke, a nothingness, all written in my stars.
Swallowing is vital, the key to knowing peace,
This tavern, just a building of which I've signed no lease.
I didn't choose my project, this ain't no place to live,
A mind with no direction, a town with none to give.
~~~Stone Ronson

Cheryl Strayed did take that hike . . . A hike that risked her life and took her over three months to accomplish. Seventeen years later the autobiographical book, *Wild: From Lost to Found on the Pacific Crest Trail*, was published.

When I first read her book, I had trouble sympathizing with her. I thought she was using her mother's death as an excuse to be irresponsible and immoral. I felt she hadn't liked herself and how could she like herself anymore by hiking?

After all, I thought, *how can a person hike to get away from her troubles and problems when SHE is the problem, and she can't get away from herself?* I also felt she was not appreciative of all the things she had been given which included, intelligence, a gift of being able to write, a loving, faithful husband, and almost having a college degree.

In my opinion, she used her mother's death as an excuse to become promiscuous, mistreat her husband, take drugs, have an abortion, and be irresponsible. And now she was going to take a 1,100-mile hike!

As I started doing research on Cheryl to use her as an example of someone who didn't like and accept herself, I started to understand Cheryl and even admire her.

What I admired about Cheryl was her blatant honesty. When she wrote her autobiography, she did not pull back any punches. She told it all like it was. People who had had similar periods of depression, grief, and despair over the passing of a loved one, are now able to get help from what Cheryl experienced.

I saw an interview on youtube.com where Cheryl said while on the trail she started to understand her mother had loved her too much for her to throw her life away. She felt her mother had sacrificed a lot for her, and she needed to honor those sacrifices by being the woman her mother had raised her to be.

 **HIGH ROAD HINT #10 – YOU CAN'T DRIVE AWAY FROM YOURSELF. SO YOU BETTER LIKE YOURSELF.**

Cheryl said she was the same on the outside before and after she hiked on the trail. She started as a waitress and when she got off the trail was a waitress again. Yet she had changed on the inside. Cheryl Strayed was no longer lost. She turned her life around. She married again. She had two children. She finished her college degree. She got a Master's Degree. She became a famous writer. She became the woman her mother raised her to be.

Sometimes the journey to liking yourself is difficult. However, you don't have to take a 1,100-mile hike to come to that conclusion. You can come to it now. Like yourself and appreciate your strengths and build on them. Look for and appreciate the relationships you have. Solid relationships are necessary to fully develop you as a person. They give you a chance to give to others and continue to grow as a person.

Cheryl didn't immediately write her autobiography. She started writing about her life in smaller pieces and began to see how it was helping others. I believe that desire to help others (be of use) made her like herself better. It was not an easy thing to write about those experiences--especially with two small children and a husband--but she did.

Cheryl's husband encouraged her to submit the book (before it was published) to Reese Witherspoon to use in a movie. Reese accepted the offer and two years later her company produced the movie and Reese starred in it as Cheryl.

Cheryl now accepts herself. Cheryl likes herself. Cheryl is on The High Road of Her Personal Life. She continues to help others as a result of her candid depiction of what she experienced after the death of her mother.

***

COMMENTS AND NOTES ON HOW TO ENJOY YOUR COMPANY ON THE HIGH ROAD AND LIKE YOURSELF.

_____

_____

_____

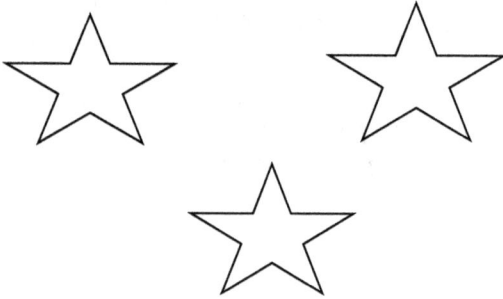

No man is an island entire of itself;
Every man is part of the main.

~~~John Donne

CHAPTER TEN - FOLLOW E.T.'S ADVICE AND PHONE HOME (DEVELOP AND NURTURE PERSONAL RELATIONSHIPS)

ET knew the importance of keeping in touch with his family and friends and having a good relationship with them. Along The High Road, it's important for you to keep in touch with your family and friends. It's even more important to get along with them.

OSMONDS - A good example of a family successful because of being able to get along with each other is the Osmond family. They started out with a quartet to raise money to buy their two oldest brothers hearing aids. From that came the Osmond Empire. It started out as trying to help.

Ralph Waldo Emerson said, "It is one of the most beautiful compensations of this life that no man can sincerely try to help another without helping himself."

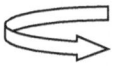 **HIGH ROAD HINT #11 – YOUR FAMILY AND FRIENDS ARE NOT PERFECT, AND NEITHER ARE YOU.**

CHRISTIAN - Batman star Christian Bale was arrested on allegations of assault made by his mother and sister only days after the $155 million U.S. record-breaking debut of The Dark Knight. His family claimed they had been assaulted by Bale at a hotel in London one day before the European premiere of the same film. He was riding the wave of his Professional Life but was on The Low Road as far as His Personal Life went. Whether he did assault them or didn't assault them, it was quite evident he was not on The Personal High Road. When his sister was later asked about the situation, she said it was a "family matter." It was reported the police let him go and didn't question him because they did not want to interfere with his movie premiere. Later it was reported Bale had gotten into an argument when his mother and sister asked him for money.

It can be very tricky to get along with members of your family-- especially those you didn't choose to be a family member. You choose your spouse, but you don't choose your parents, siblings, and usually your children.

You do not have to be perfect and neither do your friends and family. There does, however, have to be a lot of respect and love shown. I know this because of my and my own family's imperfections. Even in an imperfect world a little thing done by a friend or family member can make your day brighter.

An example of this was when my son, Stephen, sent me the following poem he wrote for me on his 28th birthday. He was born on May 13, 1984, which happened to fall on Mother's Day. On this 28th birthday, his birthday and Mother's Day once again landed on the same day.

I DIDN'T CHOOSE YOU

It's been 28 years since the first time we met,
28 years to the day.
Ten-thousand two-hundred and twenty-seven days
Of time in confluence we've shared.
I didn't choose you, you choose to have me,
Through trouble too tough for a name.
I want you to know that I'm grateful for all
Of the turmoil and all of the pain.
There's life in my bones and breath in my soul,
And it's only because of your choice.
You gave me a chance, you gave me your best,
You gave me my heart and my voice.
It only seems fitting. It only seems right
To write you this poem and say
How special I feel to have been blessed by the best,
And be born on your first Mother's Day.
God Bless you, Momma—
Your son, Stephen.

I have put together a few points to help you develop and nurture your personal relationships on The High Road in Your Personal Life.

1. WATCH YOUR WORDS AND DON'T ARGUE.

A friend of mine once gave me some good advice. She said, "Never argue with an idiot because a passerby won't be able to tell the difference between the two of you." Even responding can sometimes be construed as an argument. In those cases, it's better to say absolutely nothing. My mother always told me, "If you can't say anything nice, don't say anything at all." When we argue, whether it's with an idiot or a family member, does anyone really win? In the controversial movie, *The Interview*, it was said, "words are more deadly than a nuclear bomb."

When I heard that statement, it reminded me of a story about a father who wanted to demonstrate the power of words to his son. The father gave his son a hammer and a bag of nails and told him every time he said something to hurt his brother or sister, he had to go outside and hammer a nail in the fence. As the days went by, the son learned to control his words and not say hurtful things to his brother or sister. Soon there were fewer and fewer nails hammered into the fence. One day the father decided his son had learned his lesson so he told him to start pulling one nail out a day for each day he didn't say anything bad to his brother or sister.

Finally, the day came when the son announced to his father that all the nails were gone. The son stood proudly as he expected his father to give him an award, a present, or at least praise for accomplishing the feat. He was surprised when his father did none of those things but instead took him down to the fence. The father told his son, "I love you and am proud of you, but look at all the holes in this fence. Did you know that this fence will never be the same and this wood can never grow back together? When you use your words to hurt your friends or family, those words leave scars. You can put a knife in a man and draw it out. It won't matter how many times you say I'm sorry, the wound is still there."

This is the same thing that can happen when we use our words to hurt those we love. Even though we pull out the nails and say we're sorry, the holes are still there.

To get on The High Road of Our Personal Life, we have to learn not to argue and to watch our words when interacting with friends and family. I believe Christian Bale learned his lesson. A few years after the incident with his family and a few other bad press moments on the set of his movies, I saw several press releases and interviews about Bale visiting children in hospitals and dressing up as Batman. Maybe he was doing this to get closer to his Professional High Road, but that doesn't automatically put him on His Personal High Road.

There are a lot of people who may be driving on Their Professional High Road, but Their Personal High Road is filled with potholes and missed opportunities.

2. SHOW FAMILY AND FRIENDS UNCONDITIONAL LOVE AND ACCEPTANCE.

CARL - Going through a divorce, I decided to get an additional Master's Degree in Counseling/Psychology. I figured this would be cheaper than paying for therapy. At this point in our journey on The High Road, I feel I should share two very important concepts I learned from Carl Rogers in my college studies at that time which changed my viewpoints on how to deal with family and friends. These two concepts are "Show Unconditional Love and Acceptance" and "Perception is

Stronger than Reality." Let's first look at the Unconditional Love and Acceptance concept.

The statement below has helped me in dealing with my family and friends--especially when needing guidance in raising my children.

One of the most satisfying experiences I know is fully to appreciate an individual in the same way I appreciate a sunset. When I look at a sunset, I don't find myself saying, soften the orange a little more on the righthand corner, and put a bit more purple along the base, and use a little more pink in the cloud color. I don't try to control a sunset. I watch it with awe as it unfolds. ~~~**Carl Rogers**

Humanistic psychologist, Carl Rogers, was known for treating his clients with "unconditional positive regard." In his client-centered counseling, he accepted his clients without negative judgment of their basic worth. This is a concept that should also be used when dealing with those close to us. We should suspend judgment and treat friends and family in a way that communicates we unconditionally accept and love them. We should also show we believe when they want to change their action(s), they do not have to change who they are as a person. One of the worst feelings is to feel we can never be good enough to earn the love of family or friends.

3. REMEMBER PERCEPTION IS STRONGER THAN REALITY.

Henry David Thoreau once said, "It isn't what you look at that matters, it is what you see." If you believe you have the ability to have a successful, loving Personal Life, I believe you can. If you believe you can never have a successful, loving Personal Life, I believe you won't have it.

There once were two boys who knew a very wise man. They decided they would pull a prank on him to prove he wasn't so wise. They planned to each take a baby bird to the wise man and ask him, "Are the baby birds we hold in our hands dead or alive? If the wise man said yes, they planned to squeeze the birds to their death and prove the wise man wrong. If the wise man said no, they would pull the live baby birds from behind their backs to prove him wrong. The boys were so confident their plan would work but were surprised and amazed at the wise man's answer. His answer was a simple, "It's up to you. You hold the answer in your hands." We have within our hands what we need to have a fulfilling Personal Life because perception is always stronger than reality.

BOB - Think about what your perception of possible success for Bob. He was told his whole life how he was worthless. He was an alcoholic at 15, attended 19 different schools, and left home at 17 to become a violent meth and heroin addict who carried a .357 Magnum as he committed armed robberies.

He was diagnosed a sociopath and kicked out of the military. He spent time in prison. He was soon a divorced, homeless atheist with no money and no family or friends who would have anything to do with him.

Did you picture him later having a successful long-term marriage, owning 11 successful businesses--one of which he sold for $75 million? What about being honored as Business Person of the Year by the third largest Chamber of Commerce in the United States and being a runner-up for National Entrepreneur of the Year?

Or perhaps to be featured in such magazines as *Business Week, Reader's Digest, Inc. Magazine,* and *The Christian Post* for his numerous contributions to society? Or to write a devotional *Words for the Day* to help people get on and stay on The High Road of their spiritual lives?

The above information is all about a man named Bob Williamson. Bob was at the point of suicide when a horrible car accident introduced him to a sympathetic nurse who had different perceptions of the 22-year-old Williamson. She inspired him to shatter those walls of worthlessness, kick his addictions, and turn his life around.

I think. Therefore I am.
~~~Rene Descartes

Understanding this concept can help us from arguing with someone who perceives a situation differently than we do. If someone has a different point of view than yours, acknowledge their perception and encourage them to see the reality. As you do this, realize it takes time.

Also, realize you could be the one whose perception is stronger than reality. If you do not believe it, ask the family and friends of Bob Williamson, who gave up on him before he turned his life around.

4. IF YOU SETTLE FOR SECOND BEST, YOU GET WHAT YOU DESERVE.

A relationship based on "settling" rarely improves. You may soon find yourself living in an emotional draught that never gets the needed emotional precipitation. As discussed earlier, we can't pick our family, but we can pick our spouse. Too many times we may feel we have to have someone, and we end up settling. If you feel you have settled, then I do believe you got what you deserve. Especially--NEVER settle for someone who doesn't treat you as well as you treat yourself.

This means you must clearly communicate your needs. There are too many people in the world who have become comfortable being uncomfortable. Do not be one of those people.

If someone disrespects those needs after you have communicated them, the next step would be to have boundaries in place. These boundaries let the person know what you will and will not tolerate.

I will pass on a question a family member once asked me, "Is this present relationship the one you dreamed about as a child?" If it's not, then it's probably not the one you need. Why let someone who does so little for you continue to control your thoughts and feelings? If you have to convince this special person to care about you and treat you properly, they will only bring you down to The Low Road. You're better off driving along The High Road alone than riding with them on The Low Road.

5. DON'T CRITICIZE.

One of my favorite thoughts comes from F. Scott Fitzgerald's, *The Great Gatsby,* which is, "Whenever you feel like criticizing someone, remember they may not have had the breaks you've had in life." This is a rephrasing of the American Indian Proverb that tells us to never criticize a man until we've walked a mile in his moccasins.

Never criticize a man until you've walked a mile in his moccasins. ~~~American Indian Proverb

Criticism can take on many forms. It can be in words, but it can also rear its ugly head in how we look at someone, especially if we do so with disgust. We may communicate this through sarcasm or even through ignoring someone. Praise is always better than criticism, but even praise is not effective if it's not spontaneous or is used to manipulate or control someone's actions in a negative way.

ABRAHAM - Abraham Lincoln said, "He has a right to criticize, who has a heart to help." President Lincoln knew all about criticism. His Gettysburg Address is now considered one of the greatest speeches ever given. After he had delivered this five-minute speech to dedicate a soldier's cemetery, a London newspaper called it boring; a Harrisburg, Pennsylvania, paper called his remarks silly; a Chicago paper called it an insult to the memory of the men who had died; and another

Pennsylvania paper concentrated on the fact that there were a lot of dead horses lying around on the ground nearby.

President Lincoln was criticized for a lot of things. Since he wasn't very attractive and was gangly with big ears, many criticized him for his appearance. Through it all he was able to keep his sense of humor. When someone once accused him of being "two-faced," he replied back with, "If I had another face, do you think I'd be using this one?" Take Honest Abe's advice, and when you feel the need to criticize, figure out how to help.

When you feel the need to criticize others, consider these 4 points.

1. PEOPLE WHO CRITICIZE OTHERS OFTEN FEEL BAD ABOUT WHO THEY ARE.

Do you feel bad about yourself? Do you have to put others down to make yourself look better? If so, go back and re-read Chapter Nine, which discusses the importance of liking yourself. Always work on yourself before you criticize someone else.

2. FOLLOW THE GOLDEN RULE.

Don't do to others what you don't want done to you. Do you enjoy criticism? If you don't, why criticize others?

3. GET THE FACTS FIRST.

Make sure you have all evidence before you form a judgment on a friend or family member.

4. REMEMBER WE ARE DIFFERENT.

Remember the perception is stronger than reality concept we discussed earlier? Even if we are related to someone, or have been friends with an individual for a long period of time, we can perceive and value things in a different manner.

* * *

*COMMENTS AND NOTES ON
HOW TO FOLLOW ET'S ADVICE AND DEVELOP
AND NURTURE YOUR PERSONAL RELATIONSHIPS.*

_____

_____

_____

CHAPTER ELEVEN - AVOID ROAD RAGE
(FORGIVE)

I can forgive, but I cannot forget is only another way of saying I will not forgive. Forgiveness ought to be like a canceled note - torn in two, and burned up so that it never can be shown against one. ~~Harriett Beecher Stowe

Road Rage is becoming an epidemic all over the world. In the United States between 2007 and 2013 Road Rage went up 170% according to ABC News. It happens to men and women, young and old. If you go on youtube.com and type in the keywords "Road Rage" it will most likely amaze you on how many videos there are and how quickly Road Rage can start.

Some of the youtube.com videos I watched showing examples of road rage involved examples like these . . .

- ✓ The driver of a car in Omaha, Nebraska, trying to run over several motorcyclists by swerving into their lanes, speeding to get in front of them, and stopping abruptly. This driver even sideswiped one of the cyclists.

- ✓ A former police officer and a lawyer in California dressed in white shirts and ties rolling around in an intersection trying to get each other in a headlock.

- ✓ A woman in a large truck running down two other women in a small car, hitting their car, and getting out of her truck showing a false badge saying she was going to arrest them. She had been tailgating them, so they had made an obscene gesture to her.

- ✓ A man driving his family in North Carolina got cut off in traffic by two young men so he ran them down, which resulted in a fight with gunshots being fired.

If someone cuts you off in traffic, does it give you the right to run them down and attempt to smash them and their vehicle? If you do find yourself in a Road Rage situation, it is important to keep cool. Do not retaliate. Do not make eye contact. Stay in your vehicle. If someone cuts you off as you travel The High Road, you have to forgive them and not retaliate.

When you're contemplating holding a grudge against someone, think about how it helps you. Does it comfort you? Make you happier? Help lower your blood pressure? Make you money? I don't think so.

In a movie version of Jane Eyre I once watched, Jane forgave her aunt who had repeatedly wronged her. Jane Eyre told her, "Love me then or hate me, as you will; you have my full and free forgiveness." The Jane Eyre character understood holding a grudge against her aunt would in no way help her, or her aunt. It was distressing to me her aunt turned her face and would not acknowledge Jane's words.

One of my saddest experiences concerned a friend of mine wronged by his best friend of close to 50 years. They had been best friends since elementary school. They were closer than brothers. They started several businesses together--some successful and some not quite so successful. Another business venture came up and at the last moment my friend was left out of the deal with no warning. My friend was so hurt his best friend had done that to him he couldn't let it go. I truly felt at some time he would let go of the grudge and let his best friend back into his life. My friend died of a sudden massive heart attack before a reconciliation took place.

JENNIFER AND RONALD - When Jennifer Thompson was 22, a man raped and brutalized her for hours. She was filled with rage and wanted him to pay with his life and his soul. She reported the ordeal to authorities who did a composite picture which looked like Ronald Cotton. When several people told Ronald the picture going around looked like him, he went to the police station. He did this because he knew he did not commit the crime. He was in shock as she picked him out of the lineup, and he ended up in prison convicted of her rape.

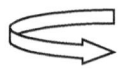 **HIGH ROAD HINT #12 – FORGIVE.**

Ronald was innocent and spent almost 11 years in prison before DNA proved it wasn't he who had committed the crimes against Jennifer. While in prison, he had already forgiven Jennifer. He needed to do that to survive his life in jail. He had to release the hate from his body.

Jennifer was consumed with guilt and shame she had misidentified Ronald as the man who had brutally raped her those years before. She was overcome with remorse she had taken away almost 11 years of his life. She finally asked for a meeting with him, and he agreed. They met in a little church building, and she asked if there was any way he could forgive her for what she had done. He told her he had forgiven her years ago. He touched her hand, and immediately she had a physical response that began the healing process for her. Because Ronald forgave her, she forgave Bobby Poole, who did commit the crime against her.

But that's not the end of the story. Jennifer and Ronald became close friends. They watched each other's children grow up and helped each other through the loss of their parents. He was there for her during her divorce, and she was there for him during his stroke and rehabilitation that left him partially paralyzed on his right side. When she remarried, he proudly attended her wedding. They even co-authored a book about their ordeal.

You may wonder how Ronald could forgive Jennifer. He said in the past all he lived for was to party. While in prison, he had a chance to reflect on what was really important, which made him a better man. He now had a wife and daughter, and the impact of the terrible situation made him more positive.

Jennifer had to not only forgive Bobby Poole, but she also had to forgive herself, and sometimes that's the hardest thing someone can do. Way too much harm has come from individuals who are not able to forgive themselves and then compensate by mistreating others Emotionally, Physically, Financially, and Mentally.

If Jennifer Thompson could forgive Bobby Poole for raping and brutalizing her and Ronald Cotton could forgive Jennifer Thompson who misidentified him and sent him to jail for almost 11 years, you should be able to forgive anyone who's done anything to you. It doesn't mean you forget it, but you can forgive it. Try, like Ronald Cotton, to find something positive about the situation that can make you a better person.

Is there a family member or friend you haven't forgiven? If so, please do something about it before it's too late. I know a lady who was a teenager when her mother died suddenly. She took her mom's death especially hard since she had continually been disrespectable, rude, and cruel to her mother. She never got the chance to ask her mom for forgiveness, and as a result had a hard time forgiving herself. I believe she still has problems with her own self-esteem because she was never able to tell her mother she was sorry and ask for forgiveness.

I often wonder about the friend of my friend who never was able to tell him he was sorry for how he treated him in the business deal. Does he wish he had apologized and would have had those precious years of friendship that were lost?

ALVIN - Whether you're the one wronged or the one who did the wrong, reconcile and forgive. Alvin lived in Laurens, Iowa, and for 10 years had been estranged from his older brother, Henry, who lived 240 miles away in Wisconsin. When Alvin found out Henry had suffered a life-threatening stroke, he was determined to reconcile with his brother before it was too late.

Alvin wanted to do the right thing, but there were several obstacles in his way. He was 73 years old, no longer held a driver's license because of poor eyesight, and did not trust any mode of public transportation. He was so determined to reconcile and make amends with his brother he left for Wisconsin on a riding lawnmower. Since he couldn't afford hotel rooms, he rigged up a mobile motel on a 10-foot trailer he pulled behind him. Five miles per hour was his top speed as he rode eight hours each day. Three days into his trip he had traveled only 20 miles of his 240-mile journey. That's when his mower wouldn't start. Still determined to clear up the difficulties with his brother before it was too late, he got the mower repaired and then drove 10 hours a day to make up the lost time.

His mower stopped again two miles from his brother's house. A local farmer helped Alvin push the mower the rest of the way to Henry's house. His journey to The High Road of His Personal Life took six weeks. As he walked up to his brother's door, Alvin didn't know if Henry would be alive or dead. He also didn't know if his brother would accept his attempts at reconciliation.

Henry was alive, but barely. As soon as Alvin and Henry saw each other there was immediate forgiveness and reconciliation. Alvin stayed with Henry until Henry recovered. Henry then moved to Iowa, and the two brothers had two good years together before Alvin died of a heart attack.

When members of the press learned Iowan Alvin Straight rode a 1966 John Deere lawnmower 240 miles to reconcile with his 80-year-old brother, they wanted to interview him--but he declined each offer. A movie called *The Straight Story* was produced in 1999 which starred Richard W. Farnsworth, who was nominated for an Academy Award and a Golden Globe for best actor for his role as Alvin Straight.

If you want to see a replica of the John Deer tractor Alvin rode, visit the Pocahontas County Historical Museum in Laurens, Iowa.

***

COMMENTS AND NOTES ON HOW TO AVOID ROAD RAGE AND FORGIVE.

_____

_____

_____

Money never made a man happy yet, nor will it. The more a man has, the more he wants. Instead of filling a vacuum,
it makes one.
~ ~ ~ *Benjamin Franklin*

CHAPTER TWELVE - APPRECIATE AND ENJOY THE SCENERY (BE THANKFUL, AND LIVE YOUR LIFE)

An old man sat outside the walls of a great city. When travelers approached, they would ask the old man, "What kind of people live in this city?" The old man would answer, "What kind of people live in the place from which you came?" If the travelers answered, "Only bad people live in the place where we came from," the old man would reply, "Continue on; you will find only bad people here." But if the travelers answered, "Good people live in the place where we came from," the old man would say, "Continue on; you will find only good people here." This Yiddish folktale shows how we find what we search for.

I finished facilitation of a week of seminars one August which started in Portland, Oregon, and ended up in Anchorage, Alaska. I was fortunate to be able to stay in Anchorage and vacation for a few extra days. I bought a train ticket to allow me to experience some of the most beautiful scenery imaginable. Would it have made sense for me to ride along in the train with my eyes closed unable to view the awesome sites outside my window? How many times do we drive through our life with closed eyes and fail to experience the beauty and joy surrounding us?

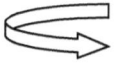

HIGH ROAD HINT #13 – LIVE UNTIL YOU DIE.

TAM - A memory I experienced on May 29, 2007, is everlastingly burned into my brain. It involved a statement my mother spoke with a wry smile, without a tear in her eyes, or a tremor in her voice to an oncologist. Her statement was, "Well then, I will live until I die." Then she turned to me and my cousin, Sandra, and said, "Where do you two want to go for lunch?"

There are so many reactions you could make when you are told you have terminal cancer. One of my beloved aunts, when she learned she had terminal bone cancer screamed so loud her husband, who was sitting outside the office in their car, heard her scream.

In this last stage of my mother's life, she never complained. She did not say, "Poor, pitiful me." She continued to live her life. Less than a month after my mother told the doctor she would live until she died, she passed away.

Mother was the most intelligent person I have ever known, and I have been around a lot of educated and smart people. She didn't have a college degree, but she was my Internet before there was an Internet. Today I can pick up my smartphone and say, "OK GOOGLE." I then hear a ping, ask a question, and usually receive the answer in a matter of seconds. When I used to call my Mother and ask the answer to a question, she would immediately give me the correct answer, no matter the topic.

Tamara (Tam) Furman Barker had a hard life. Her dad died when she was 12, and she was sent away to boarding school. After she graduated high school (barely 16) and worked for a year, she met my dad. He was poor and they remained poor for the largest portion of their marriage. Times were tough. As a family, we moved a lot, but she rarely complained. She was always thankful for her life and lived it. She never criticized me or a single decision I made. She always said, "If that's what you want to do, then do it."

After I had moved away from home, she was always glad to see me no matter how little I came home, or how long I stayed. When I promised to visit and did not follow through with my intention, she would only say, "Well, darling; I will see you when I see you." When I left earlier than promised, I heard the same, "Well darling; I will see you when I see you." Even though my mother did not have the kind of life I would have liked for her to have had, she was thankful for every minute of it and lived every minute of it until she died.

Here is a tribute my brother Ros wrote about our mother back in 2012.

This is mostly for my benefit, but I'd like to apologize to my mother. Mother, I apologize for: Not knowing what your dreams were . . . I'd bet washing dirty socks wasn't part of your dream. Expecting you to drop everything on a moment's notice because I had something I needed . . . Talking down to you . . . Telling you that "YOU JUST DON'T UNDERSTAND" when it's now perfectly clear that you did understand and only wanted to prevent the pain that you knew would come . . . Taking advantage of your trust . . . Not loving you as much as you loved your four children . . . There is so much more I'd like to say, a hundred things, a thousand things. If Tam Barker were here today, even though it is after midnight as I'm writing this with tears in my eyes, I'd call her to tell her I love her. I do. The problem with that is I'm about five years too late. June 23, 2007, was my last chance to say, "I love you, Mom." I wish this were a Mitch Albom book, and I had you FOR ONE MORE DAY.

~~~Ros Barker, Jr.

We never know how long we will have with our loved ones. Let's not shut our eyes and miss the beauty of their smiles and love. We should find ways to be thankful, and let our loved ones know how important they are to us. We should all take my mom's advice and "live until we die."

In the movie, *Shawshank Redemption*, Andy tells Red to get busy living or get busy dying. If we're not living our life and being thankful for what we have, then we are already dead.

WELLES - Welles Crowther is a young man who exemplifies the concept of living until he died. He has been called *the man in the red bandana*.

Thursday, May 15, 2014, I was mesmerized as I watched the televised dedication of the National September 11 Memorial Museum located in New York City, New York. President Obama established that day as a national day of remembrance and service, and I heard him tell a very touching story about *the man in the red bandana*. Even more touching was when I saw Allison Crowther and Ling Young hold hands and heard them speak to the crowd and the cameras. Ling was one of the survivors of the 9/11 attack on the Twin Towers saved by *the man in the red bandana*.

Welles Crowther, a 24-year-old equities trader, was the man in the red bandana. Allison Crowther was his mother. Welles is credited with saving at least 12 people by helping them down from one of the Twin Towers to safety.

He went back in multiple times to bring others as he held his red bandana around his mouth and nose to keep out the smoke. When Ling Young met him, he was carrying a woman on his back. He then asked everyone to stand who could stand and anyone who could help to help. He had found an open stairwell and led Ling Young and several others down 17 flights of stairs (with the woman still on his back) to where others were there to help them down the remaining 10 flights to ground level. Ling went down those last 10 flights to an ambulance to take her to a hospital, and the man in the red bandana went back up to help others. Within minutes, the building crashed to the ground.

Allison Crowther did not know Welles was a hero during his final moments until she saw a news story about how a lady named Judy Wein had been saved by a man in a red bandana. Allison knew it was her son because he always took a red bandana with him and had done so since he was a child to demonstrate a special link to his father.

Even though Ling Young has had to endure 30 operations to repair what happened to her on September 11, 2001, she is thankful for what the man in the red bandana did for her. One of his red bandanas is on display at the National September 11 Memorial Museum and Welles Crowther lives on in the lives of those he saved.

Here are some points to help you to "live your life" and to be more thankful.

1. HAVE A "THANKFUL" JOURNAL.

Every day, write down at least a couple of things you are thankful for. They don't have to be dramatic. Examples could be, I am thankful to see my daughter's smile, I am thankful to be pain-free, or I am thankful to have a roof over my head. When you have a bad day or feel unthankful, pull out the Thankful Journal to read some of the things for which you are thankful.

> **Be thankful for what you have; you'll end up having more. If you concentrate on what you don't have, you will never, ever have enough.**
> ~ ~ ~ Oprah Winfrey

2. THANK THOSE WHO HAVE DONE SOMETHING GOOD FOR YOU.

Below is a note of thanks, I put on Facebook after a dear friend of mine (Harold Gene "Tuck" Tucker) passed away who had been my friend for over 30 years. I only wish I had taken the time to thank him more when he was alive.

Thank you, Tuck, for being my friend and helping me get through some bad times. Thank you for being such a good friend to so many others as well. Thank you for your service to your country in the Vietnam War. Thank you for being such a good father to your son, Jeff. Thank you for being such a good son to your parents. Especially how you've helped your mother these past several years. I don't know what she's going to do without you. Thanks for being such a good brother, especially to your brother, Bobby, and taking care of his business and personal affairs after his passing. Most of all, Tuck, thank you for being you. Be sure to tell Bear Bryant up there in heaven that I said hello. You WILL be missed. God bless you and your life. I love you.
~~~Your Friend, Judy B.

When you thank someone, it can improve your mood. Enjoy the smile on the face of someone who is appreciated. Thank the person who holds open the door for you. Thank the person who brings you that cup of coffee.

Thank as many people as you can every day in every way. It is hard to be depressed or unhappy when you look for people to be thankful to.

As I fly across the U.S. to provide training and seminars, I often see service men and women. It is a joyful experience to watch the airline personnel and passengers acknowledging their sacrifices and thanking them for their service. If we fail to seize our moments of happiness and be thankful for them, they can drift away.

3. HELP SOMEONE LESS FORTUNATE.

There are always individuals less fortunate than you. Look for them and do something for them without expecting anything in return. An individual who is less fortunate does not always mean he or she has less money or fewer material possessions than you. It could be someone who has fewer friends or does not have a loving spouse like you do. Remember Welles Crowther. He gave his life helping others he did not know. What are you doing to help someone?

A young couple curiously watched an old man walking along the beach. He was gently placing starfish back into the ocean that washed ashore unable to get back into the water on their own. The young couple contemplated the large number of starfish that littered the shore and knew the old man could not save them all. They asked him why he did what he did, especially since it really didn't make that much of a difference. As he placed yet one more of the starfish into the ocean, he said, "It made a difference to that one."

We might not help everyone, but why not help those we can, when we can, where we can, as much as we can?

4. LOOK FOR SOMETHING POSITIVE IN EVERY SITUATION.

It is often difficult to find a silver lining in those dark clouds around us. Yet there are countless examples of individuals when faced with unexpected trials and dark clouds are able to find something positive that makes things better for them than what they originally hoped for.

DAVID - David Cook, planned to be a professional baseball pitcher, but threw his arm out shortly before entering college. After this disappointment and negative experience, he turned his efforts to music. He went to the American Idol audition to support his younger brother Andy and was not prepared to try out for the title of American Idol.

David Cook did not become a college or professional baseball player, but he entered the American Idol competition, won the competition, and went on to have a successful musical career.

JIM - When you find that silver lining, it requires you to believe in yourself when no one else does. Around 1990, Jim Carrey drove his old Toyota up to Mulholland Drive in the Hollywood Hills. As he overlooked the city, he wrote himself a check for $10 million and dated it Thanksgiving of 1995. He was broke and disheartened with his inability to make it big as an actor; he so wanted something positive to hang on to. It worked because by the time 1995 came around he had starred in several blockbusters and was commanding $20 million for any motion picture in which he starred. Carrey buried that $10 million check with his dad as a tribute because his dad had always supported his dream to become a star.

ANN - Ann Arnall in her divorce from her husband did not find anything positive in the almost $1 billion check she was offered. Her ex-husband, Harold Hamm, built Continental Oil from the ground up with her help. Since Ann was an economist holding executive positions in the company, she denied the amount and said she wanted and deserved more. She felt she deserved half of the $18 billion in stock and assets they had accumulated during their 26-year marriage. How much money does it take for us to find something positive in a bad situation? Later Ann did cash the check and took almost $20 million worth of property and retirement and banking accounts, saying she was going to continue to fight for more.

5. SPEND QUALITY TIME WITH FAMILY AND FRIENDS.

One of the best ways to show your family and friends you're thankful for them is to spend quality time with them. No matter how busy you are, block out time and be completely present. That means conquering the desires to do something like stare at your smartphone or text every few seconds.

A 2013 survey of 1,000 British parents indicated 95% of the parents felt the key to happiness was spending time with their family. Quality time together with family was higher on the poll than material possessions, money, or career as a key to happiness.

Have scheduled family nights. They could consist of eating pizza and playing games, or watching a movie. This shows you are thankful for your family relationship and want to continue to cultivate it.

When you spend quality time together, you can keep your family relationships strong. Relationships do not suddenly fall apart.

Several years ago a divorced friend of mine shared how her ex-husband suddenly ended their relationship with no warning. She said they had never had an argument, and she couldn't figure out why he asked for a divorce. I believe the relationship had to have started to deteriorate some time before, but she had been in denial.

A building doesn't suddenly fall to the ground, nor does a relationship suddenly fall apart. Years of abuse and neglect will cause that building to fall down. I saw a news story about Gary, Indiana, and how there were so many deteriorated buildings in their current condition because of the cold, harsh winters, and the wind off Lake Michigan. They deteriorated because no one spent any quality time with them. When a hole appeared in the roof, no one repaired it, so the hole got bigger and bigger. Then rain and snow fell inside from the hole in the ceiling, and moisture damaged the floors and walls inside. Then there were more holes, more snow and rain, more moisture, and more and more damage to the floors and walls. I saw what had once been a beautiful church building totally fallen apart from neglect.

Buildings and relationships must have upkeep, or they will erode over time.

* * *

COMMENTS AND NOTES ON HOW TO APPRECIATE AND ENJOY THE SCENERY ALONG YOUR HIGH ROAD.

Part Four –
Take The High Road
In Your Financial Life

Chapter Thirteen - Watch out for Those Alluring Exits (Use Your Head and Your Heart to Properly Balance Financial Decisions), Page 129.

Chapter Fourteen - If Your Tires are Bald and You're Out of Gas, You Can't Help Those You Meet Along the Way (It's Easier to Help Others if You Have Money), Page 133.

CHAPTER THIRTEEN - WATCH OUT FOR THOSE ALLURING EXITS
(USE YOUR HEAD AND YOUR HEART TO PROPERLY BALANCE FINANCIAL DECISIONS)

It has been said art, wealth, power, and beauty can all corrupt. Lord Henry said he chose his friends for their looks and his enemies by their intelligence. Basing decisions on your head takes intelligence. As you travel along the Financial High Road, there's always a temptation to turn off at every exit. Your heart wants you to see what is there while your head tells you to keep focused and not waste money.

DAVID - David Bach, the author of at least 12 financial books, suggests we can be smarter in our finances by having a 3-Basket Approach to financial security in his book, *Smart Women Finish Rich*. The three baskets, according to Bach, are **Security Basket** (Have at least 3 to 24 months' worth of living expenses in case of an emergency), **Retirement Basket** (Invest for growth and never borrow from your retirement account), and a **Dream Basket** (Define your dreams and hire a financial advisor with a strong support team). By doing this, you can keep your "head" when making financial decisions.

DEBRA - Debra Rogoff knows what it's like to have a battle between her head and her heart. There was no reason to suspect anything unusual about the box of Annie's Sour Cream and Onion Cheddar Bunny Crackers she had purchased. There was no reason to suspect the ethics of her and her family would soon be tested by this seemingly ordinary box of crackers. Then the moment came when Debra's daughter found out she had a special box of crackers.

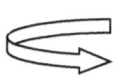

HIGH ROAD HINT #14 – WHEN MAKING FINANCIAL DECISIONS, USE A PROPER BALANCE OF HEAD AND HEART.

Have you ever wondered what you would do if you found a large sum of unmarked, untraceable money? Would you be strong enough to turn it in to the police? Or would you go on a shopping spree? If you returned the money, you would be on The Financial High Road.

What if you lost faith in the banking system and started to save your money in an envelope and hide it in your home? If you accidentally misplaced the envelope, would you be able to handle the fact you might never again see your life savings? Would you be grateful enough to thank the person or persons who found it and returned it all? Would you offer them a reward? If you were on The Financial High Road, you would.

Being on The Financial High Road means you are able to make decisions based on an appropriate balance of head and heart. I have not always had the proper balance. Being a single mother raising three children with very little financial assistance, I made too many decisions using a little too much of my heart and not enough of my head.

When Debra Rogoff's daughter found an envelope with $10,000 in cash in a box of crackers, I'm sure Debra's heart told her to go on a shopping spree. There was no way for anyone to know her family had that money. Her head told her the right thing to do was to turn in the money. It wasn't hers. So she took The Financial High Road and turned the money in.

The money belonged to an unidentified Lake Forest, California, woman who didn't trust the banking industry and had hidden her envelope with $10,000 in a box of crackers. She then returned the crackers to the store and did not remove this envelope of money.

An employee at the grocery store put the box of crackers back on the shelf, and the box with the $10,000 ended up at Debra's house. I do not believe this unidentified woman took The Financial High Road. After she had received her envelope of money, she did not offer a reward or even give thanks to The High Road Family who returned every dollar of the lost life savings. She did not even offer to buy them another box of crackers to replace the box they gave up. (After the story was public, someone did call from her family to thank the Rogoffs citing they hadn't called earlier because they thought the Rogoff family didn't want to be contacted.)

What kind of relationship do you have with money? Does the love of it consume you? Is the love of money keeping you off The High Road? Is it wrong to have money? Do you feel God looks more favorably on those with no money than those who have money? These are questions you must answer for yourself to have the proper relationship with money.

I must admit I believe there's nothing wrong with having money if it's used in the proper way. I also believe it's important to realize how difficult it is to help others if you can't even pay your own bills.

***

*COMMENTS AND NOTES ON
HOW TO AVOID ALLURING EXITS AND PROPERLY
BALANCE YOUR HEAD AND HEART WHEN
MAKING FINANCIAL DECISIONS.*

Our incomes are like our shoes. If too small, they gall and pinch us. If too large, they cause us to stumble and to trip. ~~~John Locke

CHAPTER FOURTEEN - IF YOUR TIRES ARE BALD AND YOU'RE OUT OF GAS, YOU CAN'T HELP THOSE YOU MEET ALONG THE WAY (IT'S EASIER TO HELP OTHERS IF YOU HAVE MONEY)

ED - It is not easy to stay on The Financial High Road, not even for celebrities. News headlines are filled with famous people either bankrupt or facing bankruptcy. Ed McMahon, the announcer for Johnny Carson for so many years, had financial difficulties in the last few years of his life. At one point, he was almost $500,000 behind in his house payments. Because he did not Take The Financial High Road, he was not in a position to help anyone; he could not even help himself.

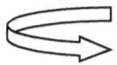 **HIGH ROAD HINT #15 – IF YOU CAN'T FINANCIALLY HELP YOURSELF, YOU WON'T BE ABLE TO FINANCIALLY HELP OTHERS.**

My financial advice for you is motivational only. I am not a financial guru, and even financial gurus can go bankrupt. My main goal is to provide motivation for you to get your financial house in enough order to be able to help others. This is the area of The High Road that is the most difficult for me as I tend to think more with my heart than with my head.

Most Americans, famous or not, have a desire to Take The High Road and help those less fortunate. They donated over $2 billion to help the victims and families of the September 11 terrorist attacks. They gave $1.54 billion to help tsunami victims in Southeast Asia and $6.5 billion to help victims of Hurricane Katrina.

MARK AND PRISCILLA - In 2013, Mark and Priscilla Zuckerberg were considered the most generous Americans when they donated 18 million shares of Facebook stock worth almost $1 billion to a nonprofit organization. That year the top 50 contributors made donations totaling $7.7 billion with pledges of an additional $2.9 billion.

BILL, MELINDA, AND WARREN - According to *Fortune Magazine*, the Giving Pledge organization, started by Bill/Melinda Gates and Warren Buffett in 2010, had nineteen members. More than 120 of the world's wealthiest have pledged to give at least half their wealth to charity.

It is much easier to help others if we have money. As a result of Taking The High Road Financially, we can use our resources to assist others. Sadly, there are many Americans who are not financially stable enough to help anyone, because they drive toward The High Road with bald tires and empty gas tanks.

Also, there are many materially wealthy people whose souls are not wealthy. They have money but feel no delight when they help anyone. Their motivation to keep full gas tanks and functioning tires is only for their own benefit.

Let's look at two individuals who not only had the money to help others but have wealthy souls.

BERNIE - A poor immigrant's son is determined to get on and stay on The High Road. He starts a business and fuels it with hard work, determination, and empathy. As his business is growing, an employee seeks his advice because her child had a disability. Unfortunately, he can't help her because he doesn't have the financial means to do so. He makes her cause his cause and suffers with her as there are few places for her to go for help. He vows never to forget what she and her child went through. Years later he retires with enough money to found an organization helping children with disabilities similar to his former employee's child. This is the epitome of the true American dream and his name is Bernard (Bernie) Marcus, who was a co-founder of The Home Depot.

During the Great Depression, Bernie was born to Jewish-Russian immigrant parents in Newark, New Jersey. He grew up poor in a tenement with a variety of excellent excuses to fail. Instead Bernie works hard to put himself through Rutgers University, graduates with a degree in pharmacy, and acquires a job in a drugstore as a pharmacist.

That in itself is a success story, but it does not stop there. He grew to love the business and retailing elements of the drugstore which led him to be involved in several retailing jobs before becoming a top executive with Handy Dan Home Improvement Centers.

Under Bernie's leadership, the chain grew to 80 stores and along the way he learned a lot about home improvement. When the Board of Directors fired him, it would have been easy for 49-year-old Bernie to Take The Low Road, but he didn't. Instead, he banded together with another employee fired on the same day named Arthur Blank to enlist investors and create the home-improvement chain, The Home Depot.

Their ingenuity of warehouse shopping and stocking to the ceiling enabled Bernie to serve as the company's first CEO, and in 22 years grew the company into a $30 billion giant. No other retailer has had this measure of success in that short period of time.

Bernie Marcus built his business by Taking The High Road ethically, using respect and generosity as anchors. His employees were never only staff; they were family. He trained his employees to please the customers by being courteous, helpful, and knowledgeable. They catered to the customer. Every executive walked the floor to talk and listen to customers. The customers repaid The Home Depot staff when they came back to buy again, and again, and again, and Bernie rewarded his employees with stock options. Over 3,000 of his employees and former employees are millionaires.

What's the significance of Bernie Marcus getting on and staying on The Financial High Road?

Back when he had no money, he worked for various charities and was only able to give his heart, soul, and time. Now he has money to give. Using his well-earned money he coordinated the opening of the Georgia Aquarium through a $200 million gift; donated $15 million to Georgia Tech University's Nanotechnology Center; created the SHARE Initiative, a program to help wounded U. S. military service members and their families get additional care; and, maybe most importantly of all, founded the Marcus Institute.

The Marcus Institute's goal is to turn "disabilities into abilities" one child, one family, and one community at a time. The Institute specializes in Autism, ADHD, Pervasive Development Disorders, FAS, and Feeding Disorders sharing its knowledge and expertise with caregivers, schools, social services personnel, and the medical community. In seven locations throughout Georgia, professionals diagnose, treat, and help children cope with development disorders.

These children now have the opportunity for a higher quality of life by learning to successfully circumvent barriers and realize their greatest potential--a chance the child of Bernie's former employee never had. What started out as an odyssey to help one child, ended up making miracles come true for more than 30,000. This dynamic and brilliant organization is the direct result of Bernie Marcus staying on The Financial High Road.

BLAKE - From the finale of *The Amazing Race, Season 2*, to building a charity shoe line, Blake Mycoskie has put his footprint on The Financial High Road. As a contestant on the reality show *The Amazing Race*, he took notice of those less fortunate he met along the way and decided to do something about it. He didn't close his eyes, ignore the poverty, and simply run faster. Because he was successful in business, he had the financial means to help.

While in college, he exercised his entrepreneurial abilities by starting an on-campus laundry service. His business was received by students in the college, and thanks to smart marketing strategies, the business expanded. He later moved to Nashville, Tennessee, where he formed the company Mycoskie Media. The company used sides of buildings as a way to advertise in Nashville and Dallas. This ingenuity led to his company being obtained by Clear Channel, and Blake was free to start a new chapter in his life.

The opportunity arose for Blake to participate on the reality TV show, *The Amazing Race*, with his younger sister. This sibling couple worked together to come in third overall for the season, only four minutes shy of winning the grand prize of $1 million. Prior to the filming of this show, Blake was the successful 25-year-old owner of an advertising firm in Nashville who had never traveled outside the United States. As he ran in the competition, he saw highs and lows of living conditions around the world and was especially touched by the need for basic necessities in South America.

After the finale, on an assumed two-week tour, Blake stayed in South America, learning how to sail in Brazil and play polo in Argentina. It was in Argentina where Blake had his revolutionary idea, *buy one, give one*. He wanted to create a shoe company for every pair of shoes sold, one would be given away.

This one-for-one concept was immediately put into action, and TOMS and the *Shoes for Tomorrow* slogan were created. The sole purpose (no pun intended) of starting the TOMS shoe brand was to donate shoes to impoverished children in South Africa and Argentina. The company reached this goal when he made casual shoes in an Argentine canvas shoe style with a sponge rubber bottom. Each pair cost around $40 back then and came in many different colors and patterns.

Blake is another perfect example of someone who took The Financial High Road. He obtained a business degree and succeeded in making wise business decisions. His creative ideas and plans of action proved to be extremely lucrative. After his time on the hit reality show, Blake merged his business and marketing strengths with his caring and compassionate nature. Blake uses his background to provide a vital need to children in poor areas of the world.

Though he had money and could afford nice things, Blake did not simply start a company to gain fame. He stimulated buyers to purchase shoes as he let them know they help TOMS do a good deed. This is what Blake believes is the reason for the great success he has seen with his shoe line. He does not ask for donations or handouts or used shoes.

In 2011, *TOMS Eyewear* was established which helps restore the sight of someone for each pair of eyeglasses purchased. In 2014, *TOMS Roasting Co.* was started to provide a week's worth of clean drinking water for those who need it for every bag of coffee sold. By the end of 2014, *TOMS* had given more than 35 million pairs of new shoes to children in need living in over 60 countries and helped restore sight to over 250,000 people in 13 different countries. Talk about "Amazing."

Even though the two preceding examples are very wealthy, do not think you have to become a billionaire to have enough money to help someone. My experience with people leads me to believe if we aren't charitable with a little money, we probably will not be charitable when we start to make a lot of money.

One morning my minister shared from the pulpit a story of a man who made a difference because he saw a need, had enough money, and was able to help. He was not a billionaire, but he gave what he had. He donated some used furniture to a family from church, who were parents working in minimum wage jobs. After receiving the furniture, they were so thankful they wanted him to come over and see how nice the furniture looked in their living room. At first he didn't want to go because they lived in a part of Des Moines, Iowa, that wasn't the most desirable area in which to live. By going there, his eyes were opened to how people lived who were less fortunate than he, so he started to serve in a soup kitchen and contribute more to those who had needs. Because he was on The Financial High Road, he had money to help out with. He took some apartments he owned and turned them into low-rent units for couples like those he had given the furniture to. If he had been on The High Road with bald tires and no gas, he would not have been able to help out when he saw the needs of those couples. Sometimes it takes money to help others.

John D. Rockefeller felt from an early age his purpose in life was to make money so he could use it wisely to improve mankind.

If Mr. Rockefeller's purpose in life is also yours, here are a few helpful hints to guide you toward The Financial High Road so you can help others.

1. START YOUR OWN BUSINESS.

If you want to have a lot of money to help others, you probably aren't going to make as much money working for someone else as you would working for your own successful business. Did you know only about 10% of multimillionaires inherited their wealth? So get out there and start your own business.

2. DON'T BE IN DENIAL.

When you are physically and mentally sick, you go to a doctor. If you're financially sick, you should also be willing to get help. Don't be in denial concerning your financial problems. There are many good financial books and magazines that can help you get back on the right track. Look for services online, but do be wary of individuals and organizations who may try to take advantage of your financial pain.

3. MANAGE YOUR VEHICLE(S).

Do you really need a vehicle? It may be less expensive to use public transportation. At a seminar I facilitated in downtown New York City, I asked for a show of hands for everyone who drove a car to the seminar. Only three out of almost 70 people raised their hand. By not having a vehicle, you will save the money you would pay for gas, insurance, and maintenance.

Do you really need to buy a new vehicle every couple of years? You might be surprised to know most millionaires drive reliable used vehicles; maybe that is what helped them to become a millionaire.

4. DON'T BORROW UNLESS IT MAKES YOU MONEY.

A good rule of thumb is to try not to borrow unless it will make you money. Also, watch what you borrow against. If possible, don't borrow against your home, retirement programs, or insurance policies-- especially to pay off credit cards. Far too frequently, we run the card balance right back up. I know that from personal experience. Instead, get a part-time job and put all the earnings from it toward the credit card with the highest interest rate.

5. USE CREDIT CARDS ONLY FOR TRAVEL AND CONVENIENCE.

Publilius Syrus (who started out as a slave to later win his freedom from his master) is credited to have said, "It is a fraud to borrow what we are unable to pay." But sometimes we may not be able to purchase what we need with cash. If you do use credit cards, make your payments on time, and keep the percentage of your income you owe under 30%.

Credit cards were first used mainly for travel to keep from having to carry cash. Maybe we should get back to that concept instead of charging even our everyday life necessities. Credit has become too easy, so it's up to you to limit what you charge and the amount of credit cards you possess. This doesn't mean you immediately close out credit card accounts, because when you close out a credit card, it hurts--not helps--your credit score.

6. BARGAIN MORE.

Don't be afraid to bargain. Remember almost everything is negotiable. If you can't get the seller to reduce the price, wait to buy when the price does come down.

7. DON'T KEEP UP WITH THE JONESES.

Don't try to keep up with that Jones family. I once read a story about a family, who to appear wealthier than they were, lived in an empty house to be able to pay the lease on a house in an expensive neighborhood. Outwardly they appeared to be keeping up with the Jones. Inwardly they lived like homeless people who slept in sleeping bags and ate off paper plates placed on the floor.

8. HAVE A BUDGET.

A budget helps you to work for and accomplish financial goals. You do not have to wait for the perfect budget. Most millionaires have budgets. They know how much money comes in and how much goes out. The success you experience when you stick to a budget can propel you into other financial successes.

9. USE CASH INSTEAD OF CREDIT CARDS.

Use cash instead of credit more often. Why should you use cash? (Remember what Publilius Syrus said.) Also, you will spend less, won't be charged interest, and won't spend when your cash is gone.

10. SPEND LESS THAN YOU MAKE.

Always spend less than you make. If you can't afford it, don't buy it. If you have a problem because you tend to spend too much, you might want to do a money personality profile. Judy Garland died $4 million in debt because her "Diva" personality led to impulsive spending habits, and she couldn't get organized concerning finances. Do you spend more when you're frustrated or depressed? If so, find out what it is in your personality which encourages bad spending practices.

Do you waste money? The U.S. Government does. The Government spent $100 million for a satellite which never made it into space. We then stored it in a closet in Maryland paying $1 million a year for rent. Is it still there today? Are we continuing to pay rent?

11. SHARE YOUR MONEY.

Look for inspiration in someone or in a cause you want to help. I have shown you examples like Helen Keller, Carl Elliott, Bernie Marcus, Blake Mycoskie, and Bob Williamson, who were inspired to help others. Be willing to not only share your time and efforts but also your money and abundance.

12. BUY USED WHENEVER POSSIBLE.

When possible, buy used. Never buy books (except one of mine), cars, jewelry, or office furniture new. It will amaze you how much money you will save in your lifetime when you buy used instead of new.

13. NEVER GET TOO COMFORTABLE.

CHARLES - Even a financial expert, who once arrived at his lectures in a chauffeur-driven white limousine trimmed with gold, can have financial problems. In the late 1980s and early 1990s, Charles Givens wrote financial books to give advice on finances and investments. One day he was sued for violating Florida's Deceptive and Unfair Trade Practices Act, and had to pay. Then he was hit by dozens of lawsuits which included a very expensive $14 million class action suit payout in California. Basically, he was sued because he claimed he used his strategies to make his money and then wrote about it when he actually made his money when he sold his financial strategies. He died in the late 1990s of cancer with his company in bankruptcy.

ROBERT AND DONALD - Another example concerns Robert T. Kiyosaki, author of *Rich Dad, Poor Dad*. His *Rich Dad* seminars were investigated in 2010 by the Canadian Broadcasting Corporation. Also, in 2010 one of his companies, Rich Global LLC filed for bankruptcy in Wyoming Bankruptcy Court. Business Mogul Donald Trump has had businesses go bankrupt, even though he has not filed personal bankruptcy.

14. USE YOUR COMMON SENSE.

A busy executive was out of the country when he got word his dad had passed away. He was not able to go to the funeral so he told his sister to plan whatever necessary for their father to have an appropriate burial, and he would pay for it when he got back from his business travels. When he returned to the United States, his sister discussed the funeral arrangements and gave her brother a statement for a very large amount of money to cover all the funeral arrangements needing to be paid. The executive paid the bill in full, but one month later he received a bill for $25 from the funeral director. He paid the bill. The next month he received another $25 bill from the funeral director. When he received the third $25 bill, he called his sister to ask why he received the same $25 bill every month. That is when he found out his sister had not used common sense; she had buried their father in a rented suit.

15. STAY MARRIED, IF POSSIBLE.

Divorce is expensive. Keep a stable relationship. Seeking and cultivating new relationships is very expensive.

* * *

COMMENTS AND NOTES ON HOW NOT TO HAVE BALD TIRES OR BE OUT OF GAS ON THE HIGH ROAD.

_____

_____

_____

LAST NOTE

I end this book with a message a wife found in her husband's jacket pocket after he had passed away. It helped him through his battle with cancer.

The message continues to help her and her son in their loss, and I hope it helps you in your lifelong journey on The High Road.

His message said:

> KEEP PRAYING.
> KEEP PLANNING.
> KEEP PUSHING.

* * *

RECAP OF HIGH ROAD HINTS

HIGH ROAD HINT #1. Make a commitment to Always Take The High Road in all areas of your life, Page 11.

HIGH ROAD HINT #2. You are never too low to get on The High Road, Page 17.

HIGH ROAD HINT #3. There's a difference between being Friendly and being a Friend, Page 27.

HIGH ROAD HINT #4. Spend time improving your situation, instead of stressing out about it, Page 35.

HIGH ROAD HINT #5. Drive the car. Don't let the car drive you, Page 44.

HIGH ROAD HINT #6. Turn Potholes into Stepping Stones to get you to where you need to go, Page 64.

HIGH ROAD HINT #7. Pave Your High Road with Respect, Rules, Resourcefulness, and Responsibility, Page 72.

HIGH ROAD HINT #8. A good leader is not afraid of failure, Page 83.

HIGH ROAD HINT #9. Beware of Workplace Bullies. They are deadly and have no respect for you, Page 86.

HIGH ROAD HINT #10. You can't drive away from yourself. So you better like yourself, Page 104.

HIGH ROAD HINT #11. Your family and friends are not perfect, and neither are you, Page 107.

HIGH ROAD HINT #12. Forgive, Page 116.

HIGH ROAD HINT #13. Live until you die, Page 121.

HIGH ROAD HINT #14. When making financial decisions, use a proper balance of Head and Heart, Page 129.

HIGH ROAD HINT #15. If you can't financially help yourself, you won't be able to financially help others, Page 133.

Other books by Judy Barker Austin

Excerpt From:
Things My Mama Said:

When Mama said, "Let's Make Slaw," I translated it to mean, "Judy--you make slaw because you need to be punished. I want you to be miserable doing something you hate to do."

After Mama passed away, I found myself thinking, *"I wish Mama were around to ask me to make slaw."*

Not that I was seeking punishment. (No I am not a masochist.) I realized when I came to Mama's kitchen and sat at the kitchen table "making slaw" was our alone time. She was usually taking the boiled potatoes out of the pressure cooker to add ingredients to and mash. Sometimes she washed a few dishes. She always asked me how I was doing and shared with me things she had been thinking about. Since everyone hated making slaw, my brother--later brothers, later husband, and later kids--gave us a lot of space. It was Mama/Judy time, and it was usually the only occasion we had private time. It was important for her to make sure we had this time to nurture our relationship.

* * *

Excerpt from The God Complex: Family Secrets:

As Peter picked up Papa's Bible to return the prayer, an envelope fell to the floor. He retrieved it, tore it open, and found three unusual keys inside. As he turned the keys over and over in this hands, questions filled his head. *What are these keys for? Why hadn't Papa given them to me before now? What did Papa mean when he said there were family secrets?*

For the first time in his life he felt weak and helpless. He realized he was not ready to relinquish Papa's guidance, wisdom, and love.

In a room nearby, Papa's private duty nurse and housekeeper heard a bloodcurdling wail and ran into the bedroom to find Peter sobbing and tightly holding Papa's frail body.

* * *

*Thank you for the purchase of this
High Road Book.*

*Look for more High Road Books now in the works
to help you stay on The High Road.*

To schedule up-to-date training and seminars for your organization or business, contact Judy Barker Austin at P. O. Box 94, Centerville, IA 52544, or judybarkeraustin.highroad@gmail.com
to schedule up-to-date training and seminars
for your organization or business.

www.ingramcontent.com/pod-product-compliance
Lightning Source LLC
Chambersburg PA
CBHW070158100426
42743CB00013B/2960